THE MIRACLE POWER OF
TRANSCENDENTAL MEDITATION

the text of this book is printed
on 100% recycled paper

The Miracle Power of
Transcendental Meditation

†

NORVELL

BARNES & NOBLE BOOKS

A DIVISION OF HARPER & ROW, PUBLISHERS

New York, Evanston, San Francisco, London

WHAT THIS BOOK
CAN DO FOR YOU

For the first time in America, the mystic art of Transcendental Meditation is being presented in easy to understand, everyday terms that you may begin to use immediately for achieving miracles in your everyday life.

This book presents the latest scientific findings in regard to meditation and the so-called Alpha brainwave techniques, which are now being investigated in universities and medical centers throughout America.

This book is a breakthrough for the layman on the subject of meditation and the Alpha brainwave methods. To obtain the best results, read this book through once and absorb the entire scope of the work. Then return to the specific chapters that will help you the most, your present needs and act upon the principles given in each chapter. Use the meditations exactly as given, either memorizing them at first, or reading them until you have absorbed their meaning. Then, when you go into your various states of meditation, think the thoughts embodied in the words, or say them to yourself softly, until you are completely in the state of meditation you wish.

There are two types of meditation: one is passive, in which you adopt a certain mental state and hold it throughout the meditation, putting yourself into the mood you wish to invoke. This type of meditation requires no words, only your thoughts, and these should be serene and calm, in what scientists call the Alpha brainwave of about eight to twelve cycles per second. This is a healing meditation and can be entered several times a day to relax your mind and body and give you immediate benefits in achieving peace and tranquility when you meet difficult challenges in your daily affairs.

The second type of meditation is positive or active. In this you project thoughts or words, and picture the results you are trying to achieve by a conscious, imaginative act. Most of these active medita tions concern such important matters as finding your right work increasing your financial security attracting love and marriage, going into business, developing creative arts and talents, and othe material and physical benefits that you are trying to attain.

The spiritual benefits from passive meditation are many. You are able to contact the higher psychic centers of your mind and receive intuitive guidance in your daily life. Through passive meditation vou can contact the higher cosmic mind, which we call God, and receive direct communication as to how you should live your life and how to attain spiritual growth and soul evolvement. In religion this form of meditation is called Prayer, and it is a simple form of communion vith the intelligence that rules the universe.

Here are some of the many benefits that you may expect from the use of Transcendental Meditation as given in this book:

1. You will immediately expand the horizons of your consciousness, giving you tremendous new insight into your own power potentials for achieving a great destiny.

2. You will be able to improve your memory and have instant recall of everything you need to guide you in your daily life. This includes names, faces, facts and details that have been buried for years in your subconscious mind.

3. You will learn how to release brainwave patterns in the Alpha, Beta, Theta and Delta ranges that show you how to have serenity and inner tranquility.

4. You will learn how to use meditation to control your body and its functions. You will control your heartbeat, your blood pressure, your digestion and be able to slow down the aging of the body cells and increase your chances for overcoming sickness and bodily pain.

5. You will be able to use meditation to increase your own mystic powers of the mind, to tap the cosmic mind and

receive psychic guidance, extra-sensory perception, clairvoyance and divine intuition. This power will help you
avoid mistakes and guide you to the fulfillment of your
perfect destiny.

6. Meditation will show you how to increase your income and
tap the universal storehouse of riches, that can shower you
with all kinds of abundance; money, houses, lands, jewels,
stocks and bonds, and all the other good things of life.

7. You will discover and use the dreamless sleep meditation
known as Sushupti, from India, in which you can overcome
pain, sickness and bodily disorders. You can stop your
dependence on sleeping pills, aspirin, tranquilizers and
other forms of drugs.

8. Meditation will reveal the method for overcoming harmful
habits. If you want to stop smoking you can do so within
two weeks or less with meditation. If you have other habits
that drag you down, you can invoke the power of meditation to assist you in changing them into positive forces for
good.

9. You will learn how to unfold the seven sacred Chakras of
consciousness that will immediately give you cosmic consciousness. This secret from the Far East helps you unlock
tremendous mental power and gives you instant control of
your mind, your nerves, your muscles and your body functions.

10. You will be shown how to use the sacred flame ritual from
the Temples of Isis and Osiris in Ancient Egypt, with their
rituals and invocations to bring your most cherished dreams
of what you want most come true in every detail.

11. You will learn about the mystical Lotus Blossom meditation
that comes from ancient Tibet. With this one meditation
alone you can invoke spiritual power that will lift you above
the physical limitations of the everyday world, and cause
you to enter into the mystical land of Shangri-La where
there is eternal peace, love, joy, and fulfillment to every
desired detail.

12. You will discover the ten stages of mystical elevation that
you may achieve by going into transcendental meditation.
You will learn how to rise above everyday problems by
ascending the spiritual mountain top. There you will dis-

cover the true cosmic power that frees you from the gravity-pull of earth that had been barring you from achieving control of any problem holding you back.

13. You will learn how to achieve astral projection through meditation, and send your soul out into the cosmic spaces at will. Up there you can meet and confer with the immortals, and bring back priceless secrets that will greatly change your life for the better.

14. Do you long to paint pictures, write stories, compose great music, invent useful objects? You can use meditation and the Alpha brainwave techniques to achieve the unfolding of new gifts and talents that can make you rich, famous and popular.

15. With transcendental meditation you can project your mind to the minds of others, influencing them for good, magnetizing their brain centers to follow your suggestions and commands. You can contact rich and important people who will help you achieve your every dream of financial power.

16. Have you ever wondered if you can overcome your problems, and have a mind that is free of worry, anxiety and fear? Through meditation and by using the dynamic brain wave pattern known as the Theta stage, you can wipe away anxiety, solve daily living problems and achieve complete conquest of fear, worry and anxiety.

17. Do you long for a more magnetic personality so you can secure your desired social life and have worthwhile friends? Meditation can help you increase the magnetic content of your brain and make you most attractive to other people. You can have powerful and rich friends who will help you attain your goals of financial independence, living in the house of your dreams.

18. Meditation is also helpful in increasing your romantic attraction to members of the opposite sex. There is a true soul mate somewhere in existence that you can attract through the use of special meditations which are given in this book.

19. You will be shown how to use meditation and perform the mystical rites and invocations that will open hidden doors to higher spiritual and cosmic forces. You will learn of the candle light ceremony, using the sacred colored flames, to

raise your spiritual vibrations to new and commanding cosmic heights.

20. You will learn of the nine mystical meditations that can be used for every purpose in life. You will be shown how to utilize this power daily to give you strength and energy, and to receive brilliant patterns of creative thought that will inspire you to a great destiny of your choosing.

This book is your lifetime program for transcendental meditation. You can use it to invoke some of the highest powers known to mankind, mentally, physically and spiritually. You can literally perform miracles for yourself through the guidance given in this book. These meditations have been proved over thirty years of my teaching metaphysics, and I can promise that if you use them, as shown you in this book, you will be enriched with benefits you may not have previously thought possible for yourself.

NORVELL

CONTENTS

THE MIRACLE POWER OF
TRANSCENDENTAL MEDITATION

TRANSCENDENTAL MEDITATION, THE MYSTIC POWER THAT CAN MAKE YOUR DREAMS COME TRUE

1

The ancient art of transcendental meditation comes to us from the mystical lands of India and Tibet. It offers humanity an amazing system of scientific procedures that can literally perform miracles for those who practice it.

In recent scientific disclosures regarding meditation and the Alpha brain-wave techniques, it has been shown that this ancient mystical art is the greatest miracle power that man has ever discovered!

THE MIRACLE POWER WITHIN YOUR MIND

You possess within your mind centers a tremendous mental, physical and spiritual power with which you can literally perform miracles in your own life. When you release this creative power through tran scendental meditation and the brain wave techniques, which we shall study in this book, you will be able to achieve, not only the healing of your mind and body, but the attainment of all your innermost dreams of happiness, financial security, right work. love fulfillment and peace of mind and peace of soul.

In this chapter we shall study the method by which you may channel the awesome powers of transcendental meditation to your own life and make your every dream come true.

THE FOURTH ESTATE OF
CONSCIOUSNESS YOU MAY TAP

Through the use of transcendental meditation you may enter a fourth estate of consciousness that is totally different from anything experienced by your normal conscious faculties.

Here are some of the astounding miracles that have been performed by scientists in medical research centers in universities all over the world: Healing powers of the body have been accelerated to such a point that reportedly tumors have been dissolved in a short time; blood pressure has been lowered to normal, when it was dangerously high, in fifteen minutes of meditation; heart action has been increased or decreased as much as five beats per minute, and patients with serious heart conditions have been greatly helped.

NEW HOPE FOR THE
SICK THROUGH MEDITATION

When you go into transcendental meditation your oxygen consumption will decrease by twenty percent. This is as much in ten or fifteen minutes of meditation as a person experiences in a full eight hours of sleep at night!

The lactic acid salt particles in the blood decrease by fifty percent in meditation. This is vitally important, for it is the lactic acids in the bloodstream that cause a person to be fearful, worried and anxious. The lactic acid salt also causes unnatural fatigue and paves the way for many serious disorders of the body.

When you go into meditation your body has a greater resistance to germ invasions, colds, viruses and other disorders of the head, throat and lungs. This was proved by scientists when they passed an electrical current through the skin of a person in deep meditation. Their machines showed that there was an increase of five hundred percent in the resistance of the current to the negative forces that might infect it, such as germs and infections of various kinds.

However, it is not only physical healing that is achieved through transcendental meditation; it can be used to treat many forms of mental illness. Scientists have used transcendental meditation to overcome drug addiction, alcoholism, smoking and other unhealthy and destructive habits. A group of nineteen men between twenty-one and thirty-eight years of age, who were heavily addicted to drugs such as LSD, marijuana, heroin and barbiturates, were put into states of meditation daily for a period of three weeks and they reportedly were cured!

WHAT TRANSCENDENTAL MEDITATION CAN DO FOR YOU

You can begin to use the power of transcendental meditation today and experience its amazing and miraculous results almost instantly.

Here are some of the things it will do for you: You will be given peace of mind and tranquility, so that your body will overcome the tendencies to diseases that come from nervous exhaustion, fear, worry and other negative emotions.

You will increase your powers of concentration so you can give all your mental energies to your work, ensuring yourself of financial security for the future.

You will improve your memory and ability to retain what you read and what you see. You can learn foreign languages, file facts and details in your mind that you can instantly recall when you want them.

You will improve your imagination and powers of visualization, so you can call up new combinations of ideas that could make you successful as an inventor, author, composer, artist or scientist. Many of our greatest creative geniuses use this art of transcendental meditation to receive their great ideas from the cosmic mind.

You will receive business ideas from your higher mind that can cause you to attract your right work, invest in the right stocks, sell more of your products, and in other ways, become financially secure.

How A Businessman Used
Meditation To Achieve Success

James E. was a typical American businessman, when I met him. He was worried and overworked. He owned a used car lot in Los Angeles, and he feared competition. His sales had dropped off and he became highly nervous and irritable. He was overweight, he had a heart condition and high blood pressure. He couldn't sleep nights from worry, so he took sleeping pills. He smoked too much and drank ten cups of coffee a day to give him pep. He became worse and worse and finally sought out my help.

I found out that not only was James E. in a very bad shape mentally and physically, but his home conditions were deteriorating rapidly. He had a wife and two children, and he was so irritable and nervous that his wife was threatening him with divorce.

I showed this man how to go into meditation, and use the powers of his higher mind. He was frankly skeptical, until after the second week of treatment, when he went to his physician and found that his blood pressure, which had been up to two hundred, was now down to about one hundred and seventy! The doctor immediately took him off the medication he had been using to lower blood pressure, thinking that it was the medicine that was causing the reduction. Frank E. did not tell him he was using transcendental meditation! Two weeks later, without medication, his blood pressure was down to one hundred and forty and the doctor found his heart action normal!

However, the greatest miracle that came to Frank E. was not the restoration of his health, it was in the new life that opened up to him in other personal departments. He was less irritable and nervous and his wife and children became reconciled to him. He was able to stop smoking entirely within three weeks of meditation, and he could sleep nights without sleeping pills. He now had so much energy that he began to give more attention to business and soon he was such a success that he opened another car lot nearby and ran both places with great success!

How To Go Into
Transcendental Meditation

1. Choose a quiet room in your home where you can be alone for at least half an hour for your first session in meditation.

If it is night, dim the lights, and have a white candle burning. Also have incense or other fragrance, for this helps the psycho-neuro brain centers achieve a state of complete relaxation during meditation.

Sit in a comfortable chair or lie on your back on your bed, with your hands at your sides, in a completely relaxed position.

Repeat the following sacred mantra from Tibet several times: Ohm mane padme ohm. This means, the jewel in the heart of the lotus, and is symbolical of the soul within man, which reflects God's eternal splendor and perfection.

2. Now breathe deeply while you say the mantra, and if you wish, say the words aloud, letting the gentle humming motion vibrate up into your head. Keep your eyes closed as you go into meditation, al-

though, later, you will learn that meditation may be indulged with the eyes wide open, under certain conditions.

3. Now mentally visualize a quiet lake that extends from the sides of your temples, engulfing the entire world. This lake is analagous to your mind. When you have a disturbed thought it will be like a ripple on the surface of the lake, disturbing its peace and tranquility. At first it is only natural that your thoughts will jump from one subject to another. Do not let this worry you, for you will gradually be able to achieve an absolutely tranquil mind. When such disturbing thoughts arise, mentally push them down, until they are once again submerged in the lake and the lake is as smooth and calm as the surface of a mirror.

When the surface of a lake is smooth, it reflects the blue sky, the sun and the trees growing at the edge of the lake. So too, when your mind is calm and still, it is a reflector of the highest spiritual forces in the universe. It is able to reflect the infinite cosmic mind that can guide you to the fulfillment of your right destiny.

4. As you hold this state of meditation and feel peaceful and quiet within, breathe deeply to the count of four. Hold the breath for a moment or so, then gently release it like a deep sigh. After you have done this breathing five or ten times you will have a feeling of elevation and mental exhiliration, which will tell you that you are now in a deep state of transcendental meditation.

This stage of meditation is known as the Alpha state. When the brain waves are measured on a machine known as the electroencephalograph, they are shown to be in the Alpha range, which is from eight to twelve cycles per second.

In this state of meditation you will feel as though there are no problems in the world. You will have a sense of deep peace and tranquility. Your nerves and muscles will be completely relaxed and under perfect control. This Alpha high, as scientists call it, is conducive to healing the body, and also opening the higher psychic centers of the mind, giving greater insight to problems and helping you achieve a sense of balance and control of all your faculties.

A Woman Overcame A Mental
Condition Through Meditation

A woman in my lecture group in New York had a severe mental shock that required psychiatric treatment. She had not responded too well to treatment and became steadily worse. She was depressed mentally and suicidal. Her husband, out of desperation, brought her to some of my lectures and heard about transcendental meditation. He began using the Alpha techniques to put her into a deep state of meditation, and from the very first session this woman responded favorably. Within a few days time, after her periods of meditation, she would drift off into a sleep-like state which lasted one or more hours. She kept up this form of meditation for a period of three weeks, experiencing benefits daily. At the end of that time she seemed to be completely cured. She reacted in a normal manner to life's challenges. She was able to stop taking sleeping pills to go to sleep nights, and drifted off to sleep within five minutes by using her meditations. She seems to be on the road to a complete mental recovery of her health.

5. When you have achieved the state of meditation known as Alpha, you can direct your mind and body to obey your every command. The autonomic nervous system controls the heart, the digestion, the blood pressure, the healing of the body, the action of your lungs. At one time it was thought impossible for one to control these automatic functions of the body. Now scientists know that one can control these functions and alleviate many of the symptoms of sickness, such as headaches, insomnia, pain and anxiety.

Give your mind commands now to control your heartbeat. Concentrate your mind on achieving a slowing down or an increase in your heart action. You will soon be able to monitor your own heart action and make it beat faster or slower. This is invaluable for people who suffer from heart ailments.

Tell your mind that you want to lower or raise your blood pressure. If it is now too high, you can control it and lower it to normal. If you suffer from low blood pressure and have constant fatigue and exhaustion, you can tell your higher mind to raise your blood pressure.

A Woman Used This Meditation
To Overcome Rapid Heart

Mrs. Florence D. was excessively heavy and suffered from high blood pressure and rapid heart. She learned in our lectures about transcendental meditation and the Alpha brain wave control. She began to use meditation every day for a period of only fifteen minutes. After her third attempt, she found that her heart, which was beating at the rate of ninety-five beats per minute, slowed down to about eighty beats per minute. Normal is about seventy-two.

At her next meditation session she was able to bring the heart action down to normal! Now she was so encouraged that she decided to tackle her weight problem. She told her mind that she wanted to lose fifty pounds. She asked her higher mind how she could overcome her craving for sweets, carbohydrates and starches. She meditated on this problem each day for three weeks, and then she noticed that she had less craving for sweets. Within four weeks time she saw that she was gradually losing weight, and in three months, with constant daily meditations of fifteen minutes, she had actually lost thirty pounds! She is now on the way to achieving her perfect normal weight through this method.

6. To use transcendental meditation for purposes other than controlling the body or healing physical sickness, the same technique for going into the Alpha state is used. However, during the state of meditation, it is necessary that you consciously guide your mind into the channel of thought you wish it to follow. When you have consciously selected this pattern of thinking, it goes into the autonomic system of subconscious control and will externalize in your outer circumstances of life as dynamic forms of action.

For example, if you wish to experience a change in your personality and you want to be more dynamic and attractive, sit in meditation and completely relax your mind and body. Then select the mental image you wish to project of the type of person you want to be. It has been found in meditation that holding visual pictures, as one does in daydreaming, tends to fix those pictures in the consciousness. Then the sympathetic nervous system projects the mental images into their physical and material equivalents.

Imagine the type of facial expression you want to wear habitually. Is it a smile or a frown that you want on your face?

Visualize yourself as popular, surrounded by a group of admiring friends, who are attracted to you because of your charm and magnetism. Then mentally take on the qualities that make for a dynamic and magnetic personality. See yourself as being considerate and kind. Radiate friendliness and warmth in your new personality. See yourself praising others and giving them your friendship. Build a mental aura around yourself of beauty, charm and courtesy. People are quick to respond to someone who is sincere and outgoing in his personality.

How A Girl Changed From Being A Wall
Flower To One Who Was Popular

Marjorie S. came into our work in California, and had a real problem in personality maladjustment. She was shy and frightened of people. She was an orphan and never forgot those lonely years as a child when she had been deprived of love. She was in a perpetual shell and froze when she met strangers.

She was twenty-two years of age and had a normal girl's dream of love and marriage, but she could not bring herself to respond to men who tried to date her.

I gave her this regimen for building a charming personality and then gave her this meditation to use every day, as she stood before her mirror to rebuild her new self-image:

> *I now create the new self-image of charm and beauty that I wish to project to the outer world. I build in my aura the quality of beauty, and I think beautiful thoughts and project them to everyone I meet.*
>
> *I now overcome feelings of self-consciousness and inferiority and condition my subconscious mind to thoughts of poise, self-confidence and charm. I love people and I know that people will love me in return. I desire love and marriage and I now meditate on attracting the true soul mate who will propose marriage to me. I am perfect and I attract a perfect destiny!*

This girl began to change gradually. She was less timid and as the meditation became caught up in the automatic sympathetic nervous system, and was second nature, she really became more beautiful, more confident and more poised. She was soon dating regularly and the last time she reported to me, she had two proposals of marriage!

7. You may use transcendental meditation to project your inner subjective dreams to the outer objective world of reality.

If you have a desire for financial independence and want to have a bigger income, you may use meditation to achieve this goal.

If you wish to release creative ideas that can make you rich, sit quietly in meditation and say or think these words:

> *I am now in the magic circle of God's infinite supply and abundance. I live in a rich universe and everything has been created for my use and enjoyment. I now project the sum of $100,000 as a life goal, knowing that I can have financial independence with this sum of money. I desire the smaller sum of*

$1,000 within two months time for my immediate needs and I magnetize my brain centers now with the consciousness of money and its equivalents.

Remember, when you use positive meditations such as this, your brain sends out electrical and magnetic impulses to your nerves and muscles. You are then motivated to do the things and go to the places where you can achieve your greatest success. Your conscious mind is limited but your higher super-conscious mind is unlimited and knows a thousand ways by which you might become rich.

How A Woman Projected $5,000 Through Meditation

A woman in our lecture work in Los Angeles used this method of meditation to project the sum of $5,000 which she needed for some specific purpose. She was in real estate but she had not made a sale in some weeks. She had listed a piece of property that was most unattractive, for one of her clients and for which there did not seem to be a buyer.

This woman began meditating on this problem as follows: "I know that there is a buyer for this property somewhere. There is no lack or limitation in God's rich universe. I shall attract the right buyer for this property, someone who shall profit from its purchase. I now relax my mind, confident that my good will come to me."

Two weeks after she began her meditation and the mental projection of the sum of $5,000 she wanted, a representative of a big oil company sought her out. He wanted to buy the old house on a corner in Los Angeles and tear it down to build a big gas station!

She sold him the property and her commission for this sale was $4,500. But, remember, she had asked her higher mind for the sum of $5,000. She was pleased with the results of her meditation, but she now kept projecting the smaller sum of $500. to make her complete $5,000. Within a week she received a letter from an uncle in Oklahoma who was quite rich, with a gift check for $500 enclosed!

8. Do you want to go into a new line of work, or own a business of your own, or have an increase in salary? Meditation can be used to achieve any of these desires.

Sit in regular periods of meditation for at least fifteen minutes a day. Go into the Alpha stage of meditation. Mentally project the work you wish to be in. See it in all its details. See your own business;

visualize the shop or store, with your name on the door, and keep meditating each day on seeing yourself in that business, being a big success.

A man in New York worked for a big firm that had several executive positions, but they were all filled. He learned about mental projection and meditation and believed in it so sincerely that he went out and had a name plate made with his name on it, which he kept in his home. At night, when he returned home from work, he sat before that sign and projected this meditation:

> *I now project this sign onto the door of an office, where I shall be working as an executive for my company. I see the increase in salary. I concentrate on the comforts and security it will bring for my family and myself. I am confident that this promotion will come to me in the immediate now.*

Within one month, one of the executives was retired from the firm, and out of ten other prospects, the man who had been meditating on promotion, and being an executive, was chosen for the position. The sign he had made for his office was put up and the reality he had projected through his meditation was now a fact!

9. You can use transcendental meditation to project trips you want to take, people you want to meet, romantic situations you wish to be in, and material objects, such as cars, furs, jewels, stocks and bonds, houses and lands — in fact, any material possessions you desire, can be projected to the Cosmic mind, and they will gradually materialize their physical equivalents for you.

To project such material things sit quietly in the Alpha state of meditation and think or say the following words:

> *I now project these physical and material images of what I want to attract in the future. I wish to meet interesting and important people socially, who can help me further my social career and lead a life of pleasure and emotional satisfaction.*
>
> *I wish to attract my future soul mate for purposes of matrimony. I know that somewhere this perfect mate exists and I now invoke the law of magnetic attraction which will make my romantic dream come into glorious focus.*
>
> *I desire material objects that are the equivalents of riches, such as jewels, cars, houses and lands. I project these dreams to the cosmic mind that knows how to bring them into full realization. I visualize these objects being mine. I mentally*

possess the deeds, the stocks, the money in the bank, that can give me future financial security and make me rich.

After you have given yourself each of these above meditations for a few moments each day, have the faith to believe that these things are on the way to materializing for you.

You can make out a list of the things you wish and take it into meditation with you and then meditate a few moments on each desire. You can frame your own words and mental pictures for the different things you want, for your needs are different from any other person. Make your statements brief, positive and charge them with emotional intensity as you meditate, and see the things coming to you with perfect expectation of your good.

How A Young Man Won A Job With The Studios In Publicity Work

Harold R. was a student of mine in Hollywood who was working in an advertising agency writing copy. He was a college graduate, and desired promotion and more money, but how could he go about it? When he learned about transcendental meditation he began to go into daily meditation, at night, just before going to bed, of half an hour, visualizing and projecting himself into a job in some big studio in publicity. He visualized that this would be work he enjoyed, in glamorous surroundings, and meeting people of quality and interest. He projected a salary of $200 a week.

After two weeks of this constant meditation, Harold R. got his job, but it was not in a big studio in publicity. It was with a Los Angeles newspaper, in the copy department, writing up similar ads to what he had been doing in the advertising agency. However, he received his $200 a week that he had mentally projected.

But Harold R. did not stop projecting his ideal job picture. He did not know how, but he felt somehow he would win out and be hired by a studio eventually.

After two months on his new job, he met the editor of the theatrical and movie news, and went to lunch with him and a man who worked in one of the biggest studios in Hollywood. During the course of the luncheon this man, who was a publicity man, the head of his department, remarked that they needed an assistant in his department who was used to writing publicity stories, and did the editor know of anyone? This was the change Harold R. had been waiting for. He told the man of his qualifications, and was given an interview at the studio and got the job! His salary? Exactly what he had been projecting! It was a strange, round-about way to get the job, but sometimes it works in this manner.

Summary of Chapter One

1. How you can use the miracle power of transcendental meditation to achieve health, happiness, and prosperity.

2. You may enter the fourth estate of consciousness where you can tap powers that are higher than your own conscious mind and achieve absolute control of your mind, your heart, your blood pressure and automatic functions of the body.

3. The miraculous things that transcendental meditation can do for you, in improving your memory, increasing your imagination and unlocking creative power that can make you a genius.

4. A businessman, Frank E. was able to achieve outstanding success in his business within a few weeks time, when he learned how to unlock the miracle working power of his higher mind through meditation.

5. How you can go into the Alpha wavelength of brain control through the use of meditation and how it helps you achieve instant peace of mind and great mental power.

6. How you can overcome problems and achieve freedom from worry and other negative emotions by going into the meditation known as the spiritual lake.

7. A woman used this meditation to overcome heart trouble, obesity and other afflictions that bothered her mentally and physically.

8. How you can use transcendental meditation to make your personality more magnetic, dynamic and forceful, winning for yourself friends and business opportunities.

9. A girl used these meditations to overcome timidity, fear and anxiety, which had made her a wallflower. Within a few weeks practice she had two proposals of marriage!

10. How you can project your inner dreams of financial security and independence to the outer objective world through these transcendental meditations.

11. A woman used these meditations and projected the sum of $5,000. Within a short time she sold a piece of property and her commission and another gift brought her the entire sum.

12. How to use meditation to go into your own business. A man using this method, projected himself into a job as an executive with his firm over ten other prospects.

13. How to use meditation to project your dream of material things such as cars, furs, jewels, stocks and bonds, and houses and lands, and achieve these things with effortless ease.

14. The meditations to use for becoming rich and successful, and for attaining your true soul mate.

15. Harold R. tried these meditations to win a certain job in the publicity department of a big film studio. He was successful and made the exact salary he had projected.

HOW TO PROGRAM
YOUR NEW DESTINY
THROUGH THE POWER ─┼─ 2
OF TRANSCENDENTAL
MEDITATION

Are you living a life that you did not really choose and which you do not like?

It is possible that you are, for ninety-five percent of the people do not choose events in their lives but let events choose them.

You possess a higher mind within your consciousness that knows how to guide you to your right destiny. This higher mind may be contacted by going into transcendental meditation and asking it to guide you.

Through meditation you may be guided to the right work you should be doing. You can receive direct information as to how to effect changes in your life: where you should live, and how you can accomplish the things you desire.

How Negative Mental Programming
Affects People

Most people are programmed negatively from the moment they are born. They inherit a whole set of conscious and subconscious mind motivators which create their destinies. Most of these mind programmers are produced by the mass consciousness over the centuries and change only when you learn how to go into meditation and re-program your higher mind centers with a whole new set of mental, physical and spiritual values.

Joe G. had been programmed since childhood to believe that he would be poor all his life. He was born on a farm in the South, to a family that worked as share croppers for a wealthy plantation owner. Because he was black, he had been programmed to believe that he would have to be inferior and uneducated all his life; he was told that white men had all the money; that he could never rise above the lowly circumstances of his birth.

Joe G. was finally drafted into the army and came to New York city where he happened to drift into one of my lectures at Carnegie Hall. He had never heard about meditation, mental programming or metaphysics before, and he was instantly impressed with the fact that anyone, no matter what his circumstances of birth, lack of education or other negative conditions, could change his destiny and attract anything he wished in life.

He sought me out after the lecture and asked me how he could use transcendental meditation to help him build a new life. He was leaving the army in a short time and planned to return to his home and follow in the poverty-stricken footsteps of his family in the only life he knew.

I showed him how to go into meditation; how to reach his higher mind and ask it for guidance. I explained to him that no one had to tell him how to be born, but that this most important event of his entire life occured entirely without his conscious awareness or as-sistance. Some higher power spoke to him in the mother's womb and told him how to be born.

I further explained how this wonderful cosmic mind takes over and meets all our needs after we are born. This power does not stop work-ing when we come into the outer world, but works even better when we know how to release it. There is waiting for the new-born baby a fountain of milk, chemically arranged to nourish and sustain his body, by a cosmic chemist that knew all the secret ingredients to put into that mother's milk. I asked him, "Can you not trust such an intelligence that knows more than you or any other living human being?"

This was the beginning of a complete transformation in the life of Joe G. He left the army, returned to New York, where he continued his studies in mystic philosophy with me, and soon he was working, and waiting for the guidance that would tell him how to fulfill his destiny.

Each day I told Joe to meditate for at least a half hour on his future destiny. I showed him how to take a slip of paper into meditation on which he wrote:

What work am I best suited to?

How can I attain an education?

Should I go back to my home or remain in New York?

While he sat in meditation nothing seemed to come through, but Joe had a feeling of great calm and certainty that he would be rightly guided to his destiny.

One day when he was visiting the public library on Fifth Avenue Joe saw a list of occupations that he could be trained for through a veteran's assistance program that was being operated by the city. On the list he saw a school that trained veterans to become veterinarians. Something in his mind clicked instantly into place when he read that announcement. As though a computer in his mind had suddenly unlocked secret and hidden data, he was carried back to his days on the plantation when he had loved animals and was able to overcome many of their distempers without the aid of a doctor. He knew in that instant that he wanted to become a veterinarian!

Joe enrolled in the school, and with a loan that was advanced by the veteran's organization, he completed his education. He did not return to his hometown but set up an office in a nearby community and became one of the finest veterinarians in the business!

YOU CAN BE ANYTHING YOU WISH TO BE

By using the amazing power of transcendental meditation, you can literally become anything you wish to be.

You can mentally program your higher mind by going into the various stages of meditation, as you will learn in this book, and quickly, almost overnight, attain the mental power to change the circumstances of your life. As you form your mental habits, so your mental habits will form your new destiny.

How Meditation Brought this
Girl Success in Marriage

Two years ago a young lady came to me and told me how miserable she was. She said, "All my life I have been told by my mother that no man would ever marry me. Her life was made miserable by my father, who had affairs with other women and finally divorced her for someone else." Then she told me how she had become so convinced that she would never marry that she had never dated, although she was then twenty-two years of age.

I put this girl into a regimen of meditation at once, in which she was to begin picturing her soul mate. She was told to visualize the ideal man, with qualities of kindness, gentility, fidelity and emotional stability. Then I told her to repeat to herself over and over the following statements as she held this picture of permanent marriage and love in her mind during her meditation periods:

> *I am in the magic circle of God's protective love. It is my destiny to attract perfect love. I know that my soul mate exists and that I shall attract him by invisible cosmic cords of divine love.*

She was to repeat that statement of cosmic law five times. Then she was to sit in meditation and build her future dream home with her soul mate. She was to see herself entertaining her friends there; she was told to choose the number of children that would bless her marriage and to make them a reality by seeing them as real children; then she was to repeat the following positive statements to break the negative mental programming that had held her enslaved to the thought she could never have love and a perfect marriage:

> *I now break the mold of past mental programming. The experiences of my mother in no way affect my future destiny. I am an independent being, capable of actions of free will and I now choose the events that shall make up my destiny.*

This girl went into this type of meditation for half an hour a day for one week. Nothing happened at first. She reported to me every day by telephone, but she felt better, more light-hearted and with a feeling that something wonderful was going to happen.

The second week of her meditations the miracle began. A salesman came into her office and, as if attracted by a hidden magnet, walked over to her desk, smiled and introduced himself. She said later she knew instinctively this was the man of her dreams. They began to date the next day and within three months time she married this handsome man who turned out to be everything her dream lover had been!

TAKE THESE TEN SIMPLE STEPS TO PROGRAM YOUR NEW DESTINY THROUGH TRANSCENDENTAL MEDITATION

Step No. 1. Invoke the law of cosmic order in your life daily through meditation. When you go into the stillness say to your confused mind, "Peace, be still. Be still and know that I am God." This statement of positive force, from the Bible, helps focus mental and physical power.

As you still your mind and put your mental house in perfect order, mentally file all your worries, anxieties and fears into a mental filing cabinet, where they will no longer clutter up the neat appearance of your mind. As you clear this negative debris from the field of mental action you will have a feeling of calm and a sense of harmony within yourself.

How a Man Increased His Income Through This Form of Meditation

A man came to see me once who told me that his business was steadily losing money. He said, "Things have gotten out of hand in our office. Orders are delayed, papers mislaid, confusion is rampant. We are steadily going into the red and I don't know what to do about it."

The man was highly nervous; he would start and stop in his speech, twist his hands, move his body and show signs of general agitation. I know the symptoms only too well: mental confusion and complete disorientation, which often precede a complete nervous breakdown.

After listening to his long story of how his home life had deteriorated and that outbursts of temper with his wife and three children had caused him to seriously consider suicide, I knew that this man had reached the end of his mental rope and was about to take the final desperate plunge into oblivion to end his mental and physical misery.

I instantly put this man into the Alpha state of meditation, where his brain waves were slowed down to from eight to twelve cycles per second, by telling him to visualize his mind as being a peaceful lake, and his troubled thoughts as ripples or waves on the surface of the lake. Then he was to mentally push down each little wave until it was submerged in the body of the lake. When all the waves had been removed by this mental process his mind would be as calm and still as that lake, which could now reflect the blue heavens above, the golden sun and the green trees beside the lake.

Soon a tranquil expression came over this man's face. Then I took him deeper and deeper into meditation, until he was completely calm and tranquil. I gave him a series of positive mental programmers to repeat whenever he became confused, and he was to say these five to ten times each until he achieved the stillness of the Alpha lake exercise:

I am in a state of harmony and peace. I now project order into my environment. My thoughts are under my control. They are peaceful, calm, loving, joyous and confident. I am as cool and calm as that lake and my mind is in perfect balance and order.

Within three weeks time this man reported to me again. He was a changed man. His first words were: "A miracle has happened. I have stopped worrying, I don't lose my temper as often as I did, and since I put my mind in order, I seem to have more energy than ever before. Now my office seems to be more orderly and even my wife and children seem to respond with more love and understanding."

This man did not understand the miracle that had occured. As his mind became orderly and calm, his environment took on the qualities he brought to it, for life is like a looking glass, it will reflect whatever is put before it.

Step No. 2. When you start your day's activities sit for five minutes in meditation and program that day's activities. Make out a list, like you do when you go shopping, and list the various actions for that day.

If you are a salesman program that you will make five sales for that day.

If you are a housewife, program yourself to a day of peaceful action, positive emotional values and joyous experiences with your family. Program out of your mind anxiety, worry and fear by dwelling on the positive forces you wish to invoke for that day.

If you are in your own business, program that day's income, the sales your employees will make, the general atmosphere of success you wish to maintain and the level of service your establishment shall maintain.

Step No. 3. Each day, while in meditation, build the cosmic magnet of success and abundance. This is done by magnetizing your brain centers with all the facets of success, mental, physical, material and spiritual.

As you sit in meditation pass each success thought through the filaments of your brain, very much as electric current is passed through the filaments of an electric light bulb. This tends to magnetize your thought currents with whatever emotional charge is in your mind.

Dwell on success in all its many aspects. See yourself making money and buying the things you want. Visualize your body being healthy and strong. See yourself attracting friends and having their love and respect. Visualize the dream house or apartment you want to live in. Mentally project the sum of a thousand dollars and affirm several times in meditation, "This money will come to me from unexpected sources."

How A Woman Magnetized $1800 More
Salary For Her Husband Through This Method

A letter from a woman in San Diego told me of how she had magnetized the sum of $1800 more a year for her husband. I had given a Demonstration Lecture in that city and told of this method of working miracles through meditation. She began to work on projecting this sum of money for her husband. He was called into the manager's office just two weeks later and told that his name had been entered with those of three other men for a raise of exactly that amount!

Step No. 4. Before going into meditation write down a list of the ten things you want more than anything else in the world. Your list might look like this:

I desire the following things:
A. A new job, with the salary I want.
B. I would like the sum of $500 from unexpected sources.
C. I want to take a trip to Europe for my vacation.
D. I want to attract the right friends and have the type of social life I enjoy.
E. I wish to develop creative gifts and talents, such as painting, writing, music, composing and inventing.
F. I desire happiness in love and marriage.
G. I want to go into a business of my own.
H. I would like to get new ideas for promoting my business and making more money.
I. I would like to improve my personality and become more magnetic and attractive.
J. I would like to overcome the habit of smoking.

A young man who began this regimen in meditation put down such

a list of ten things he wanted to occur in his life. Within two months
five of them came to pass, and he is now confidently working on the
other five. When you achieve several of your objectives, change the
list and meditate on other things you wish to happen in your life.

Step No. 5. Take into meditation a regimen of positive mental
habits that you wish to build and program them into your higher mind
centers daily. This schedule can be a daily regimen which might look
like this:

Mon.   Today I shall invoke the law of divine order and harmony
in my life. My thoughts and actions are all in accordance with order,
harmony and balance.

Tues.   This day I shall clear up all unfinished business in my
mind and my environment. I shall write those letters I have put off.
I shall approach the client I want to sell. I shall begin overcoming my
wrong eating habits and go on a diet to lose weight.

Wed.   Today I shall meditate on the good that I expect from
life. I am expectant of my good from many channels. I see every
situation as ultimately leading to good, no matter its present negative
appearances. My mind is now molded with the image of pleasant
experiences and goodness.

Thurs.   This day I shall meditate on beauty in all its many forms.
I am aware of inner spiritual beauty that radiates from my soul and
blesses every person I meet. I am conscious of the overpowering
beauty in nature and I am in harmony with the mystical forces that
create the majesty and wonder of nature, with its multi-colored flowers,
its graceful trees, its magnificent oceans, rivers and lakes. I am one
with this pageant of loveliness.

Fri.   I shall meditate today on the emotion of love and its effect
on my life. I was created in the magic circle of divine love and I
express love all day to every person I meet. God is love, and this
knowledge banishes the negative effects of hate, jealousy, suspicion
and unfriendliness.

Saturday.   Today I shall meditate on the virtues of morality,
charity and kindness. I strive to conduct myself on a high moral and
ethical basis, knowing of the cosmic law of balance and harmony. I
give to others of my joy, my smiles, my encouragement and praise
and in turn I receive friendship, love and happiness. I strive to perfect
my personality and achieve idealism in all facets of my being.

Sunday.   In my meditation today I shall dwell on the mystery back of life, the nature of God, the human soul and the purpose behind this mystical journey through time and space. I am aware of my oneness with cosmic mind and I now respond with faith in the power and with joy and wonder at the miracles that express themselves in my daily life.

A girl of twenty put into practice this regimen for a period of three weeks. She meditated each day on one of the above statements, and she later reported to me that her life suddenly began to reflect more harmony, peace and beauty than she had ever had before.

A man of sixty, who lived in the awareness of age and sickness began to meditate on this daily regimen and soon his fears dissolved and he actually said he felt twenty years younger than previously.

Meditation clears the mental and spiritual channels and puts you into direct harmony with the higher cosmic mind power that knows what you should do every moment of your life.

Step No. 6.   Knowledge is power. Each day make it a point to program into your higher mind centers some new form of knowledge that you may use to shape your future destiny. Learn a new word; memorize a poem, write a short essay on love, or friendship, or beauty. Try to draw or paint a picture from nature. Study the current scene and know wnat is happening in various parts of the world. As you meditate on higher knowledge your brain centers will become magnetized with a new sense of power and it will add immeasurably to your life experience.

Step No. 7.   Each day program into your higher mind centers positive emotions and break the mold of past negative thoughts and habits.

Meditate on confidence for a few moments and program your subconscious with this emotion. Repeat four or five times: I have confidence in myself and my future. I am created perfect. I now express that perfection in my personality, my work and my daily life. I overcome the negative emotion of fear and know that I am surrounded by God's protective circle of light, power and good.

Do the same thing with the emotions of good, peace, forgiveness, tolerance, love, kindness and charity. As you meditate on each positive emotion in turn and program it into your consciousness the habit of being positive will be formed and you will gradually break the mold of past negative thoughts.

Step No. 8.   Program each day a sense of your true value and build the self-image of poise, confidence and magnetism in your personality. This meditation can be done before your mirror just before you go out for your day's activities. Say ten times, "I was born for a great destiny. I am going to give something of great value to the world today and I shall receive in return rich rewards of money, friendship, fame, joy and satisfaction."

A famous concert singer I gave this secret to, stood before his mirror and sang up and down the scale, "I am a great singer." He did this ten or fifteen times and it seemed to help him project a quality of greatness in his voice that made him most successful.

A girl who had been programmed to think she was plain and not attractive to men used this technique in meditation and it changed her from a wallflower to a completely new and dynamic personality. She said out loud, as she looked into the mirror: "I have a secret. I am beautiful and I am beloved." She began to act as though she were a great beauty, and soon she created such an aura of beauty in her personality that people thought she was most attractive.

Step No. 9.   Use the Lotus Blossom meditation each day to give your mind a sense of lofty purpose and an elevation of spirits. Visualize a beautiful lotus blossom attached to you at your side; see it at the three foot level for everyday inspiration. The Lotus is the symbol of beauty, spiritual perfection and the soul's reflection of God. When you want higher levels of inspiration for creative work such as writing, composing music, painting, or inventing, meditate on the lotus in the five foot position. As the lotus is elevated your mind will follow suite and your spirits will be inspired to create in the image of its beauty and perfection.

Use the six and ten foot elevations of the lotus for extreme inspiration, for love, for magnetism, for spiritual power, and for meditating on the supreme mystery back of life. The ten foot elevation of meditation is when the soul knows its true spiritual ecstasy and blends with the light, in what is known as the finding of nirvana or the absolute.

Step No. 10.   Infuse your higher mind with the power of faith. Realize that your faith can heal you of any negative condition in your life. Say to yourself ten or fifteen times. "My faith shall make me whole." Until you really believe that you can accomplish anything you wish in life.

A college student approached every examination with dread, certain he was going to fail. He passed with low grades until he changed his mental programming and just before each examination he repeated ten or fifteen times, "I shall pass these examinations with high grades." He began to improve immediately for his faith released the higher knowledge of his subconscious mind where all knowledge is stored and he graduated with the highest marks in his class.

Review of Chapter Two

1. How negative mental programming affects you and how you can change it to positive programming that gives you a new set of mental, physical and spiritual values.

2. How Joe G. programmed himself into a complete new life experience and overcame the negative programming of poverty, lack and limitation.

3. How to use the miracle working power of transcendental meditation and become anything you wish to be.

4. How a young lady used this power to overcome a negative childhood in which she believed no man would ever fall in love with her. In a short time she won perfect love and had a joyous marriage to her true soul mate.

5. How to invoke the cosmic law of order and harmony in your life through meditation on the positive forces of life.

6. A businessman overcame his problems and his desire to commit suicide through meditation, and by learning how to go into the alpha state he was able to overcome his problems and make a greater success than ever.

7. How to build your personal magnet of success and abundance and magnetize and attract into your orbit everything you desire.

8. How one woman magnetized and demonstrated the sum of $1800 a year more salary for her husband through this technique.

9. The positive daily schedule for meditation in which you set up a weekly regimen to help shape your future destiny.

10. How a girl of twenty programmed her life to bring peace, harmony and beauty into her daily activities.

11. How to program higher knowledge into your mind centers to add to your sum total of complete knowledge.

12. How to emotionally charge the batteries of your mind with

positive values through positive emotions, and how you can program negative emotions of fear, worry, hate and limitation out of your subconscious mind.

13. How to give yourself the mirror treatment to overcome self-consciousness, inferiority and inadequacy and replace these with self-confidence, poise and a new self-image of power and dynamic magnetism.

14. The lotus blossom meditation to give your mind a sense of lofty purpose and elevation of spirits. The four positions of the lotus blossom for every purpose in life.

HOW TO EXPAND YOUR CONSCIOUSNESS AND ENRICH YOUR LIFE THROUGH MEDITATION

3

Many young people today are striving to achieve an expanded consciousness through the use of drugs, and they may attain some degree of consciousness expansion, but it does not last and can actually be injurious to the brain and body.

However, there is a method by which you may achieve an expanded consciousness and higher powers of the mind, without any danger to your health and sanity.

In this chapter we shall explore these methods and show how you may achieve dynamic mind power and enrich your life through simple mystic methods of control and meditation.

THE FIVE STEPS OF YOGA CONTROL FOR MIND EXPANSION THROUGH MEDITATION

1. Go into a state of meditation as explained in Chapter 1.

2. Control the thoughts by choosing one thought at a time and concentrate all your powers of mind on that one thought.

Control your nerves and body by holding still for five minutes at a time. Look at a spot on the wall and direct all your mental and nervous energy to that spot, saying to yourself: "I now control my thoughts, my nerves and muscles and assume the statue pose in which I concentrate all power and energy in my body and mind."

3. Purification and regeneration is the third step for mind expansion and elevation. This is done through a special form of breathing which helps purify the blood stream and releases the proper chemistry of brain and body.

Breathe slowly through the nostrils to the count of four. Hold the breath to the count of four, then push in your diaphragm and expel the breath in one count.

This is a tranquilizing, healing breath and should be used whenever you wish to clear your mind of negative debris and fill your body cells with magnetism and electricity. This energizing and purifying breath should be done at least ten to fifteen times and may be repeated three times daily.

4. Dedication is the fourth step in mind expansion. Each morning when you awaken, do the above breathing and then give yourself a dedication ceremony which will unite you with the source of all power back of life.

A TIBETAN MONK'S SECRET
OF LIFE REGENERATION

I once met a Tibetan monk in the north of India, from one of the great lamasaries beyond the Himalayas. He carried a prayer wheel with him on which he had inscribed hundreds of prayers to the deity. Each time he turned the prayer wheel these prayers ascended to God. He then told me the secret of his youth and vitality, for he was past one hundred years of age and yet looked and acted like a man in his early fifties.

> *Just as this prayer wheel causes hundreds of prayers to rise each time it is turned, so too I dedicate my breath each morning when I awaken to the cosmic spirit of God. As breath is the first gift He gives us, and the last one He takes back, it is important to look on breathing as one of the most vital forces in mental and spiritual regeneration. Each morning when I awaken, with my first breath I say a prayer of thanksgiving for another day of life and then dedicate each breath for that day to God, as a living testimonial to His Power, Majesty and Might. In this way each time I breathe, I am being recharged with dynamic life energy. This is the secret of my vitality and life force.*

5. The next step for consciousness expansion is elevation or absorption in the light.

Sit in meditation and visualize a mountain in the distance, rising majestically from the plains, then mentally ascend that mountain, starting with the awareness of the lowlands through which you must first traverse.

This represents the physical basis of man's existence, his body, his appetites, his desires of the flesh. As man spends ninety percent of his time in being aware of this plane he becomes more and more engrossed by his body's needs, by physical pain and sickness, age and death. His mind, when on this limited plane alone, is concentrated on making money, paying bills, being possessed by possessions, and he cannot soar into the higher realms of inspiration and glory.

Only when man is able to release himself from this earthbound existence and soar into the illimitable realms of imagination is he able to obtain freedom from life's burdens and cares.

How A Woman Achieved Freedom From Cares

A woman came into our lecture work in New York city, who showed all the symptoms of fatigue, boredom, anxiety, inability to concentrate, that indicated she was mentally earthbound and mentally, as well as physically sick. She told me how she was caught up in the minutia of life; cooking, washing dishes, shopping, taking care of three children, and never being able to relax from her chores for a moment.

I gave this woman a regimen for consciousness expansion in which she was to sit in meditation each day for fifteen minutes and ascend the spiritual mountain top. She was to rise first to the level of mind, and each day concentrate on building some interest in mentally stimulating ideas. She was to take an idea from some book on philosophy, psychology or the Bible, and concentrate on its meaning. She was to learn a poem or a new word each day, until her mind was a storehouse of interesting ideas.

Then on the next week she was to ascend to the next level of the spiritual mountain top, the imagination, and bring into focus some new and interesting ideas in the realm of imagination, such as seeing herself going on a trip. She was to do this each day for that week until she had strengthened the power of her imagination and could run through her mind many imaginary scenes in which she projected herself, thus freeing herself from the drudgery of her work-a-day world.

Then as the last stage of her climb up the spiritual mountain top, she was to meditate on the most beautiful things she had experienced in her life, beautiful scenes she had witnessed, beautiful flowers, soaring classical music, high ideals and spiritual concepts of God and the soul. This was the last stage of her ascension to the spiritual mountain top, and the most important, for it would carry her high above the limited mortal mind valleys of daily drudgery and boredom into the spiritual stratosphere of an expanded consciousness and her awareness of the cosmic wonders in the universe.

The changes that came over this woman in two months were truly amazing. First of all she lost the appearance of age and fatigue that had been so prominent before. Then she reported to me that her work did not seem so burdensome, for now her mind was occupied with her meditations as she worked, and she had the inspiration and knowledge that through her physical efforts her husband and children were being given the comfort and well-being which made them strong, healthy and happy.

But the most amazing thing of all was that as she projected mental pictures of herself through her imagination, these things actually began to happen in her outer experiences. When she projected herself on a mental trip to Hawaii, she had no thought she would ever go there, but her husband suddenly got a big bonus from his firm and they took a second honeymoon to that beautiful island!

USE THIS REGIMEN FOR ACHIEVING AN EXPANDED CONSCIOUSNESS THROUGH MEDITATION

1. Sit in meditation and concentrate your mind power on the rich, wonderful new experiences you wish to attract.

If you want to enrich your life, put rich thoughts into your consciousness. If you want to create magnificent paintings, write great novels, or compose beautiful music, meditate on the highest ideals that have been achieved by mankind in the particular field that interests you. For musical inspiration listen to the music of Beethoven, Chopin, Mozart and Handel, while you sit in quiet meditation. The soaring beauty of that music will become caught up in your consciousness and weave its tapestry of dreams for you to emulate in your own life.

How A French Composer
Uses This Method

A young composer I met in Paris a few years ago uses this method to compose magnificent music. He absorbs, concentrates, and then in meditation he creates the magnificent symphonies which seem to flow from his finger tips as though from celestial heights. He has had tremendous success and is only twenty-eight years of age, proving that one need not be old or experienced to do great things.

A young girl I met in New York had need of $1,000 for some specific thing she wanted to do. I told her to go into meditation on the spiritual mountain top and project the money as a reality. She was to imagine herself having it; she was to count it and then see herself mentally spending it for whatever she wanted. Within three weeks she had the money and it came to her in the most unexpected way from a source she had never thought possible. Her father owned some stock and had given her and her sisters a thousand shares each, but the stock had gone down and down until it was only worth a few cents a share. The family had put it into a trunk and forgotten it. One day this girl had a desire to clean out an old trunk she found in the basement, and when she saw the stock she asked her father if she should throw the certificates out. He checked with his broker and found they were now worth one dollar a share. She had her $1,000 and in the most mysterious manner!

2. If you want to increase your good or enrich your pocketbook, sit in meditation and project the good, the money or the wonderful experiences you desire. Climb the spiritual mountain top and meditate on the reality of the things you desire. Visualize yourself attracting the experience you want, see yourself meeting the people you want for friends, mentally see yourself achieving the goal you have set for yourself, or doing the work you feel should be yours. As you sit in meditation say to yourself quietly and with faith, "I now rise in consciousness to my rightful domain and achieve every good and beautiful thing that God desires for me and my life."

3. To banish loneliness, to win friends and love, to acquire thrilling life experiences, sit in meditation and elevate your mind to the planes of inspiration and beauty. Affirm to yourself, "I am encircled by an aura of friendship and love. I magnetize friends and loved ones. I

project beauty, inspiration and love and I become a magnet attracting to myself that which I now hold in consciousness."

How a Woman in Athens, Greece
Used This Formula

One day after a talk I gave in Athens, Greece, a worried looking woman sought me out and wanted to talk to me about her problem. She was from Scotland and was having her holiday visiting the Greek Islands. She told me she had lived a life of loneliness without love, and she was now certain that she could change the negative trend of her life, after hearing my positive philosophy. "But how?" she asked me, a note of desperation creeping into her voice, "I am past thirty, and am afraid of men, especially foreigners." I gave her a little ritual she was to perform each day to overcome fear and then showed her how to project the aura of beauty and love in her personality. She was taking the boat to Rhodes the next day, and when she returned, I saw her once again, and her face glowed with an inner light that transformed her features and made them almost beautiful. She said, "Your formula worked. I began to concentrate on being friendly and desirable and I met this man who was a retired officer in the British Navy. His wife had died and he was lonely. We struck it off awfully well and he wants to see me when we return to England."

4. As you go into daily meditation concentrate your mind on beautiful, inspiring and idealistic thoughts. A good way to do this is to write down brief quotations about love, joy, peace, beauty, friendship, happiness and good, and then in meditation run these through your mind, letting their full import and meaning lodge in your consciousness. Just as you become what you eat, so too you become what you think most frequently.

This exercise in meditation in the Far East is known as opening the petals of the sacred lotus. The lotus is the symbol of perfection and represents man's spiritual being. In meditation silently unfold each petal of the lotus, ascribing a different astral color to each petal. For instance, on one day let the lotus petal be the quality of love; hold the astral color of rosy pink in consciousness, then see the lotus opening revealing all its cosmic colors to your inner eye. Then meditate in turn on all aspects of love; love of man for woman; love of family, love of country, love of God. As each aspect of love is held in consciousness be aware of its meaning. Do the same with each of the above qualities, meditating each day on a new word, and adding those words or states of consciousness which you particularly wish to express in your life.

How a Woman Used This Method
To Improve Her Life

Mrs. Wilma J. was in a perpetual state of agitation and anxiety. She worried, she was cross and irritable, nothing seemed to go right for her. I gave her this exercise in meditation. She began to meditate on serenity, joy, radiance, and goodwill. Within exactly two weeks she reported to me that she had overcome most of her disturbances through that exercise. She meditated only fifteen minutes a day and changed her mental filters daily, giving each new emotion its own astral color, some sunlight yellow; others mauve, gold, viridian green, azure blue and orchid, and she said that as she meditated on each emotion and each color they seemed to soothe her mind and her emotions became serene and controlled. Now we know that this ancient practice from India and China and Tibet, practiced by monks in their monastaries, has scientific credence, for in modern color therapy scientists find that some colors are harmonious and healing, while others, like red, purple and indigo blue can be in turn, irritating, arousing anger, hatred and violence, while others, like deep purple, can cause a person to develop psychotic symptoms if looked at for a period of several hours.

5. When you go into meditation it is also a good thing for you to occasionally take a mental inventory of what thoughts are there and then have a good mental housecleaning.

Clear out the debris of negative thoughts, fear of failure, accident and sickness. Erase from consciousness the thoughts of lack and limitation, or that there is poverty in the world and supplant in meditation the positive thought that God's universe is filled to overflowing with good, that there are riches and abundance, and that God created all these gifts just for you. This will help your mind build on a solid base for future positive action.

How Problems For a Man Created by
False Beliefs Were Overcome

I met a man once on the plane going to Chicago whose face bore the evidences of negativity and deep anxiety. In talking to him, I found out that his wife was sick, his only child, a girl, was in the hospital, he was returning to be with them, although he had to interrupt a very important business trip to do so. Then, in talking to him further I discovered that this was nothing unusual. His whole history was one of sickness, accidents and misery. He had been brought up in a negative environment when he was a child, and everything was counted in terms of before an operation or after. Time was measured in the calamities that had befallen members of the family. "Was that before or after Aunt Martha fell and broke her hip? Did we do that before or after Grandpa died?" I call such persons B.C. and A.D. personalities; before calamity and after disaster.

I corrected this man's thinking, and told him that events in our outer lives are accurate reflections of our inner states of consciousness. An effect is always produced by a cause, and if the causes are negative then everything in our outer conditions of life will be negative, but if we condition our minds with positive, happy, loving thoughts, the circumstances of our lives will change accordingly and become positive.

I then showed this man how to meditate on the positive values of life and minimize the negatives. He had a heart condition, also high blood pressure; he suffered from indigestion and thought he might have ulcers. I told him how in medical research in all the big universities, through using meditation to produce the healing alpha brain wave states, people were being healed of heart trouble and high blood pressure. He had never heard of these latest scientific advances, but he was instantly excited over the tremendous implications of what I told him.

We exchanged cards and I told him to keep me posted as to his progress. I heard from him again in one month. He told me that he could hardly believe the good things that had happened since he began to go into daily meditation.

His blood pressure had dropped from nearly two hundred to a normal one hundred and forty. His indigestion had disappeared and his doctor could not believe it when he next tested his heart — it functioned normally! He said, "This can only be called a miracle. Even my wife and daughter show amazing benefits from your meditations. God bless you!"

Review of Chapter Three

1. The five steps to take to achieve Yoga control through meditation for expansion of your consciousness.
2. How to achieve control of thoughts, nerves and body movements for perfect concentration and dynamic mind power.

3. Purification and regeneration through dynamic Yoga breathing to remove fatigue acids and poisons from bloodstream.
4. How to achieve the state of dedication which elevates your consciousness to high levels of inspiration and action.
5. A Tibetan monk's secret of life regeneration; at the age of one hundred he had the body and alertness of a man of fifty.
6. How to achieve the state of meditation known in the Far East as absorption in the light.
7. The spiritual mountain top meditation which elevates your consciousness above the earthbound, mortal mind realm, into the lofty spiritual stratosphere of power, long life and health.
8. How one woman achieved freedom from anxiety, worry and fear through daily meditation and overcame many problems.
9. How to go into meditation and enrich your mind with power, riches, new experiences and anything you wish to attract into your destiny.
10. How a young French composer uses this method of meditation to compose magnificent music and achieve great success.
11. How one young lady attracted $1,000 through the spiritual mountain top meditation.
12. How to use meditation to banish loneliness and attract friends and loved ones that can make your life a joyous experience.
13. How a woman I met in Athens, Greece, was able to overcome timidity and loneliness through meditation on love and attract a retired naval officer who fell in love with her.
14. How to meditate on the qualities of love, peace, joy, beauty, good and friendship, and through opening the petals of the sacred lotus, bring each of these qualities into focus on the screen of your mind, making them a reality.
15. How Mrs. Wilma J. overcame her problems and worries by using the mental filter system of astral colors in her daily meditations.
16. How to clear out the debris of negative thinking in your mind and erase all thoughts of lack, limitation, sickness and poverty.

17. A man I met on a plane going to Chicago overcame high blood pressure, heart trouble and many home problems through a fifteen minute a day regimen of meditation in the alpha state.

HOW TO HELP YOUR BODY'S HEALTH THROUGH MEDITATION AND THE ALPHA BRAIN WAVE THERAPY — 4

Meditation has been found to be a miracle worker in healing the body and keeping it healthy and functioning normally.

Here are some of the miracles that have been observed in the laboratory of the medical colleges throughout America.

Through the system of ancient Yoga meditations, it was found that the human brain releases mysterious brain waves that profoundly affect the body's functions.

When the meditation entered the Alpha state, it was measured on the electro-encephalograph as being in the range of from between eight to twelve cycles per second. This state of meditation gave a sense of peace and tranquility. It caused the brain and body to relax, and sent mysterious forces to the heart, nerves and muscles which caused the body to heal itself of some of the most serious disorders known to science.

For the first time in centuries medical science now knows, what the Yogas of India taught over five thousand years ago — that through meditation, the mind can control the autonomic nervous system and regulate the heartbeat, the blood's circulation, the operation of the lungs, the glands, the digestion and the blood pressure.

This scientific breakthrough is now being called one of the greatest miracles of the twentieth century and with it science now believes we may overcome most disease, heal most forms of mental illness, and better still, prevent the erosion of age and premature death by actually retarding the death of the cells in the brain and body!

How a Woman Conquered Her Allergies Through Meditation

Alice G. was afflicted with numerous complaints; she suffered headaches that did not yield to medicines. She had allergies that caused her intense suffering, nasal congestion, with attendant sniffling, sneezing and paroxysms of caughing, where she could hardly get her breath.

A friend who knew of our work sent her to a series of classes I was giving on Meditation and the Alpha brain wave techniques for overcoming illness.

I described in the class how physical illness often has its origin in mental and emotional disorders, and that some hidden cause existed mentally back of most diseases. Then I showed the class how to go into meditation to induce the healing states of mind known as the alpha state.

Alice G. began her meditations the following day, and each day for half an hour she worked on creating the right mental and spiritual atmosphere for her body to heal itself. She worked for two weeks before she noticed any results. Then she told me that she noticed she was less tense and nervous. Her headaches stopped first; then she began to notice that her coughing and sneezing decreased. Within two months time she reported that she felt better than she had ever felt before and that her allergies had definitely shown signs of stopping altogether!

HOW TO GO INTO THE ALPHA HEALING STATE OF MEDITATION

No matter what your own physical complaint may be, trust your higher mind to heal your body. The intelligence that created your body in nine short months, with its miracle of chemistry and ingenious systems of nerves, muscles and blood vessels, is still in existence in the cosmic memory bank of the universe. You can only invoke this higher spiritual healing agency when you completely remove your own worrying, fretful conscious mind from the scene of action.

To go into the Alpha healing state of brain wave control, sit quietly in meditation and still your mind. You can begin this process of meditation by using the ancient Mantra from Tibet, "Ohm mane padme ohm." Say it aloud ten to fifteen times with your eyes closed. You can create an atmosphere for meditation similar to your own private shrine, with a candle burning, a sacred relic or cross before you, and a fragrant incense burning or some sweet smelling scent in the room. This helps elevate the psycho-neuro centers of the brain and releases the mind from stress and strain.

Then as you sit in meditation invoke the mental image of the spiritual lake, in which you mentally project the picture of a beautiful lake without a ripple on its surface. Now mentally see your mind as that lake. Hold the image of stillness and let your mind and body become peaceful and still. The moment a worry, fear or negative thought arises in your mind, it is as if a wave had risen on the mental lake. Carefully push the ripple back down into the body of the lake and say a quiet statement to yourself;

> *My mind is now as still and peaceful as that mental lake. I am now submerging all my cares and worries in the body of the lake. I overcome all tensions and bodily pains. The creative healing power now flows from my higher mind centers to my body and I am being healed of all discord and disease.*

When you have achieved a state of perfect inner stillness you have released your body from the pressure of worry, fear and other negative emotions. It is then that your brain waves begin to work on the body's glands, causing them to release the correct chemicals in the right proportion, and once again causing your body to be healthy.

HOW WARTS WERE REMOVED
ON CHILDREN'S HANDS

An article in one of the country's leading national magazines recently told of how psychiatrists had used this technique of meditation to remove the warts from the hands of twenty children between the ages of 10 and 12.

The children were told to draw the pictures of their warts on a piece of paper, in the exact location that the warts were on their hands. Then this piece of paper with the drawing of their palm and warts was burned in a ritual, while the psychiatrist recited an invocation consigning the warts to oblivion and stating they would disappear through the magic power released by the ritual.

The children observing this ritual believed that their warts would go away. Within a period of three or four weeks the warts on all their hands had completely disappeared!

HOW ALPHA BRAIN WAVE MEDITATION
HELPS HEAL HEART TROUBLE

The heart is one of the most responsive organs in the human body. When one is frightened, the blood rushes to the internal organs, the heart beats faster and adrenalin is pumped into the blood stream. If the emotion of fear can cause the heart to beat more rapidly, then the opposite emotions of peace and calm should have a totally opposite effect on the heart.

How a Woman Controlled Her Rapid
Heart Beat Through Meditation

A woman who came into our classes in New York city suffered from a condition in which the heart would race to as high as one hundred or more beats per minute. The normal heart rate is approximately seventy-two beats per minute.

When trying to go to sleep at night she could hear her heart racing; she found herself visualizing all kinds of calamities. She broke out in a cold sweat and often had to rise from her bed and sit in a chair half the night to avoid the panic that came from her condition.

When this woman learned how her mind could control her heart action, and went into meditation for the first time, she was delighted to find that her heart actually did respond to her thoughts.

I told her to form a fist and pump her hand, opening it and closing it, as she sat in meditation. She was to visualize that hand as being her heart. She was then to direct her thoughts in meditation to her heart with the opening and closing of her hand to the rhythm she wished her heart to beat. She was to say to herself: *My heart is now responding to my mind. I think heart and my heart reacts. I now direct my heart to beat at the rate of seventy-two beats per minute.* She was then to count one — two — three — four, until she had established the rhythm she wanted her heart to beat. She accomplished this in two sessions of fifteen minute meditations. She soon had such power over her heart that she could increase or decrease its beat at will!

How Yogas In India Regulate
Body's Metabolism

In India Yogas use this method of mind control to regulate their body's metabolism. They can stop pain at will; they can run sharp stilletos through their cheeks, arms, chest and other parts of their body and completely control the flow of blood and stop all pain. They can be buried alive for days without food or water, just barely breathing, and hold their life force in a suspended state of animation, without suffering any ill effects.

How a Woman Used Mind Control
to Regulate Her Body Weight

One woman I knew in Los Angeles who studied these alpha brain wave controls in our classes was fifty pounds overweight. She learned how to go into meditation and control her metabolism. She told herself over and over, as she quietly held her mind in a deep state of alpha suspension:

> *I shall now gain control of my body and regulate my metabolism. I desire the loss of fifty pounds of my body weight. I shall control my desire for carbohydrates, sweets and starches. I want to regain my former figure and I now command my higher mind to regulate my body metabolism to keep me slender.*

This woman repeated this affirmation ten to fifteen times in each session of meditation. She meditated three times a day for fifteen minute periods. At first there was no noticeable change in her condition. After three days she found she had less desire for sweets and fattening foods. She then found after meditating for one week that she began to eat less meat and more vegetables. Something told her to eat brown rice. She began a rice diet, with vegetables and she told me that within one month's time she had lost twenty pounds. She felt better, her mind was clearer and she lost all kinds of side effects that her obesity had produced, such as fatigue, headaches, muscular aches and pains and rapid heart when she walked.

Later when she had shed fifty pounds she had a physical check-up and found that her body was in perfect health. She told me she could never have had the mental strength to stay on such a rigid diet without the power she obtained from her daily meditations.

How a Smoker of Fifteen Years Stopped

It seems incredible that there has been no known cure for cigarette smoking all these years! Despite the fact that doctors now know cigarettes produce cancer, high blood pressure and many other diseases of the lungs and circulatory system, no one has come up with a sure cure for smokers to stop their habit.

One man in our lecture group in New York had the smoking habit for fifteen years. He heard me tell in public lectures how twenty smokers and nineteen heroin addicts had stopped their habits after a few weeks of daily meditation.

This man started his meditations by going into the Theta state, which slows down the brain waves to approximately four to seven cycles per second. This is the brain wave state that is used for memory retention, for slowing down the mental process, and also for overcoming negative habits.

I told him to visualize an hour glass with the grains of sand running through it one at a time. He was to slow down his mental rhythm to an extremely slow rate, so as to fix in his consciousness the thoughts he wanted to imprint. Then, when his brain was slowed down, he was to count backwards from number fifty to one, until he had achieved a slow rhythm. Then he was to meditate as follows, thinking these thoughts and saying these words slowly to himself:

> *I wish to rid myself of the noxious habit of smoking. I am aware of the harmful effects smoking has on my heart, lungs and general health. I wish to live a normal, healthy long life, and I realize this is impossible if I continue the harmful habit of smoking. Every time I smoke a cigarette I shall be aware that I am giving up valuable years of my life. Cigarettes are harmful to my health and peace of mind. They will taste bitter and I shall feel a sense of nausea every time I reach for a cigarette*

This man did this meditation for a period of two weeks daily for fifteen minutes, before he began to notice any difference. Then one day, after his morning coffee, when he lit a cigarette and took a few puffs, it tasted decidedly bitter. He could hardly finish the cigarette and when he did he felt a sudden sense of nausea. The reaction against cigarettes was so pronounced that within one more week he had lost all sense of craving for them and completely stopped smoking.

How a Woman Addicted To
Sleeping Pills Overcame the Habit

Pauline T. was a lecture member in Los Angeles who became addicted to sleeping pills. She would often lie awake for half the night, conjuring up all kinds of mental phantoms which kept her from sleeping. She obtained a prescription from her doctor for sleeping pills and she used them for six months, but gradually their effects wore off and she kept taking more and more, until one night she awakened to find that she could not remember how many pills she had taken. This so frightened her that she decided to do something to overcome this habit. She remembered how many people had died of overdoses of sleeping pills, and she sought me out for advice.

I told her that the fact she could not sleep showed she was deeply disturbed mentally over some emotional problem. She admitted that she had broken off with a boyfriend who had been going with another girl. She was too proud to call him and admit she was wrong, so this preyed on her mind night and day.

I showed Pauline how to go into deep meditation through taking ten or fifteen long, deep tranquilizing breaths. Then I gave her the type of statements she was to make to her mind while she was in meditation:

> *I shall now fall into a deep, natural and refreshing sleep. My mind is still and peaceful as a lake in the midst of a silent forest at midnight. I am surrounded by a sea of calmness. My mind is now retreating through the corridors of time back into timelessness. I am once again a child, without worries or cares on my mind. I have faith that God will protect me and solve all my problems. I am now floating on a cloud, up — up — up, into realms of forgetfulness, peace and beauty. I now sleep, sleep, sleep.*

Pauline completely stopped the sleeping pill habit in three weeks time with this meditation, and reported that she now fell asleep the moment she entered into her meditation and slept naturally and awakened refreshed every morning.

AUTONOMIC SYSTEM CAN BE
CONTROLLED WITH MEDITATION

The autonomic nervous system, which controls such functions as the heartbeat, blood pressure, digestion, healing and glandular secretions does not ordinarily respond to conscious control. It has been thought that the only way to reach into the subconscious, which has control of these automatic functions of the body was through auto-suggestions or through using hypnotism. However this has been found to be ineffective in many cases. Now, with the new brain wave therapy and through meditation it has been found that the higher mind centers respond readily to automatic conscious control. This is the entire basis for spiritual or faith healings, where miracles are performed when a person believes that a higher power is going to heal him.

The miracles of Lourdes are a reality and now science realizes that when anyone puts his mind into a certain state of faith and confident expectation, miracles are possible.

How a Man Overcame High Blood Pressure

A man in my New York lecture group was overweight and suffered from high blood pressure and heart trouble. He lost his temper easily, fought with his family and co-workers and did not know how to overcome the problem that was threatening him with premature death.

When he began to use meditation and put himself into the Alpha state he began to notice improvement within two or three days. By the time he had reached his second week of daily meditations he found that he could send himself into the Alpha state of meditation at will whenever he felt a fit of temper coming on. I told him at such times to close his eyes for a moment, and visualize his blood being like a red ball at the base of a thermometer. When he became angry that red ball would climb up the thermometer to the top and burst. This was the danger signal of what was happening to him as his blood pressure rose.

He began to practice this mind control and soon he could enter into the Alpha state of peaceful meditation at a moment's notice. Within three weeks time he went to his physician and had his blood pressure taken. It had dropped from a perpetual two hundred to one hundred and fifty! While the doctor watched, this man demonstrated how he could control his blood pressure at will, and he mentally projected the red ball up the thermometer until it had reached an alarming two hundred!

How a Sixty-five Year Old Woman
Overcame Low Blood Pressure

Another instance of blood pressure imbalance was a frail woman of sixty-five, who suffered from chronic fatigue and who thought her diet or age was at fault. Her heartbeat was slow, irregular and almost imperceptible. Her blood pressure fell to 115. She feared death, and worried about her condition. She learned how to go into meditation in one of my classes and began to use this method every day to send her blood pressure up. Within one week she had amazing results and her health improved. Not only did she have more energy, but she overcame many symptoms she had, such as irregular beating of the heart and her temperament became more optimistic, cheerful and outgoing. Her blood pressure rose to normal and she maintained this for many months without change.

THE REGIME FOR BODY CONTROL
THROUGH MEDITATION

1. Each day put yourself into the Alpha brain wave pattern by closing your eyes several times a day and going into a few moments of meditation. Repeat to yourself the words: "Be still, and know that I am God." Then keep telling your mind to remain still and peaceful.

2. Then visualize the spiritual lake extending from the sides of your temples and encompassing the whole world. Then mentally submerge your worries, fears and anxieties into the body of the lake until it is perfectly smooth. Now see your mind as the surface of that lake, like a mirror, reflecting the blue skies and the golden sun.

3. Breathe deeply ten or fifteen times giving yourself the following meditation, saying the words to yourself or aloud:

I am peaceful and still. My problems and worries are now submerged in the cosmic lake where they are being dissolved and returned to their native nothingness. I am serene in the midst of life's worries and my mind now reflects the golden light of God's Infinite Presence. I am surrounded by the magic circle of love and peace and beauty and I am free, free, free.

4. If you are suffering from some physical disability, and you feel that some organ is affected, go into quiet meditation and then direct the life intelligence and blood to go to that organ healing it perfectly. If it is the heart, say to your higher mind: "You will now cause the blood to flow to my heart, carrying its life force there and healing it perfectly."

If it is the kidneys or gall bladder or stomach, use the same technique, changing the words to fit your particular needs. You do not need to know the location of the gall bladder or other organs of the body; your higher mind knows their location and will respond to your directions to send the life force to whatever organ you wish to stimulate.

5. If it is a bad habit that you wish to overcome use the same technique that was given for overcoming the smoking habit.

If it is a problem of heavy drinking, go into meditation and say the following statement:

> *I realize drinking excessively is harmful to my health. I wish to lose all desire for alcohol. I now urge my higher mind to cause me to lose all liking for alcohol in any form. If I take a drink I shall find the taste unpleasant and put it down at once.*

If it is a problem of gambling, sit in meditation each day for fifteen minutes or so and repeat the following statement:

> *I know that gambling is destructive and unproductive. You cannot get something for nothing in life. I now ask my higher mind to rid me of the desire for gambling.*

6. To raise the body's energy level and overcome fatigue and aging, go into meditation and mentally elevate yourself to high levels of creativity by visualizing yourself doing the things you desire, such as swimming, dancing, playing tennis or golf. Give your higher mind commands such as this one:

> *The life force flows through my mind and body cells, giving me youth, energy and a superabundance of vitality. I now order my higher mind centers to release the chemistry of youth within my body. I am ageless and timeless and my soul is immortal. I shall live to be one hundred years of age with all my faculties and a zest for life.*

How an Eighty-five Year Old
Man Overcame Age

Frank L. was chronically ill from what his doctors called senility and symptoms of old age. His family had thought seriously of entering him into a rest home for the aged, but a neighbor who had been to some of my lectures in New York urged them to bring him to one of our meetings on meditation and brain wave therapy. Fortunately, they did, and they were amazed at how interested the old man was as he listened to the incredible tales of how people had overcome all

manner of sickness, debility and old age symptoms through meditation and the miracle power of brain wave therapy.

I had said during the lecture that an old person must not keep
pounding mentally on the fact he is old, but to reverse the cosmic
time clock and see oneself as getting younger. I told the story about
Jack Benny and how he jokingly referred to himself as being perpetually thirty-nine, and how even into his seventies he was making
people laugh and earning a fortune each year.

This story so impressed Frank that his son, later told me, he returned
to their home and set his cosmic age at fifty. He began a period of
daily meditation and affirming his cosmic age, he started to walk each
day, and visit friends nearby. He cultivated a hobby, and was soon
mowing the lawns, tending the flowers and making little toys out of
wood for his grandchildren. Within three months time Frank L. was
like a younger man and he never did return to his sick bed and his
chronic mental habits of thinking himself old and useless.

Pointers to Remember in Chapter Four

1. Meditation is a miracle working power if you have faith
   that it can keep you healthy and give you long life and
   energy.

2. Through meditation the brain releases mysterious brain
   waves that profoundly affect the body chemistry and keep
   it healthy or make it sick.

3. The autonomic mechanism of the body which regulates
   heartbeat, blood pressure, digestion and glandular secretions
   can be controlled through Yoga meditation.

4. A woman overcame allergies and bronchial disturbances
   by going into daily meditation. Her headaches stopped and
   she was healed perfectly.

5. How to go into the Alpha meditation to gain control of your
   body's automatic functions and control heartbeat, blood-
   pressure and digestion.

6. How warts were removed from the hands of twenty children
   through this method, and by building the children's faith in
   the fact their warts would disappear in a short time.

7. How this method of alpha meditation was used to heal heart
   conditions by controlling the mind and sending the blood and
   life force to the heart.

8. A woman was able to overcome rapid heart beat and achieve a normal heart beat of seventy-two beats per minute by daily meditation.

9. Yogis in India control pain, overcome bleeding from open wounds, and are able to regulate their body's metabolism through meditation and mind control.

10. One woman was fifty pounds overweight and used meditation and the alpha state of brain waves to lose weight and reduce her hunger pangs.

11. How a smoker of fifteen years overcame his harmful habit entirely through meditation and was able to achieve freedom and better health.

12. A woman addicted to sleeping pills was unable to sleep without their aid until she learned how to use meditation to go to sleep instantly.

13. A lecture member was able to reduce his blood pressure from two hundred to one hundred and fifty entirely through meditation.

14. How to direct the life force to any sick organ or part of the body and achieve a miracle healing through meditation.

15. How to overcome drinking, gambling and other bad habits through the power of meditation.

HOW TO BUILD A POSITIVE, HAPPY LIFE THROUGH DYNAMIC LAWS OF MEDITATION

5

All life is controlled by a pattern of invisible cosmic laws which man must obey, if he wishes to find happiness and success.

When we violate the laws of health and overeat or overdrink, or dissipate, we suffer consequences in bodily discomfort and sickness.

When we cheat, lie, steal or commit moral infractions of the cosmic laws, we are punished by mental anguish, illness and accident.

There is an ancient law from the Far East called the law of Karma. This law decrees that we shall be rewarded for every good thought and act and punished for every wrong deed we commit.

We can set into motion the effects we wish to achieve in our lives by instituting the right, positive causes. Then we begin to experience the immediate benefits of this great Karmic law in our lives.

In this chapter we shall study the dynamic Karmic laws that exist in the universe and see how we can benefit from them by invoking the right state of meditation for their full execution.

How a Woman Violated
Karmic Laws and Suffered

A woman came into our work in Los Angeles who told me a harrowing story of mental and physical anguish because she had violated these cosmic laws.

She had been happily married for ten years and had never cheated on her husband. She had three children and was a devoted housewife and mother. However, one summer while on a trip, she met a man who attracted her and she submitted to his advances. She later regretted her emotional indiscretion and broke off seeing this man. However, Karma was at work to punish her for her violation of moral and spiritual laws and she soon discovered she was pregnant! Now she faced a real problem, for she could not be sure if it was the result of her affair or from her husband. She could not make up her mind what to do and she sought me out for my advice and counselling.

I told her she had broken a cosmic law and that the suffering she was going through was a result of her indiscretion. She would have to face the future with the knowledge that the child might be the result of her temporary affair, and she could never wholeheartedly know the truth. This would only add to her mental and spiritual agony over the years.

"But should I tell my husband and almost certainly lose his love and respect?" she asked.

"If you do tell him and he divorces you," I said, "You can almost be sure the courts will award the children to him and you will be left with only the child from the result of an affair with a stranger. I do not think this is wise." Then I explained to the distraught woman that she could not afford to reveal her indiscretion to her husband, and risk the breaking up of her happy home. She had made a mistake; she would have to live with that mistake the rest of her life. This was sufficient Karmic punishment to wipe away the evil thing that she had allowed to happen.

This woman followed my advice. She did not obtain an abortion, for it was against her religion to terminate the embryonic life. She made up her mind that she would make it up to her husband and children by loving them and serving them in the future. She would accept the coming child as part of her Karmic duty and lavish as much love and affection on him as she did on her other children.

This decision proved right, for when the time came for her child to be born, it was a still birth. Her husband never knew the truth, but in this woman's heart and mind she must forever bear the cosmic guilt and Karmic suffering for the human error she committed.

MOST OF LIFE'S MISTAKES
CAN BE AVOIDED

When we learn how to use the dynamic laws of meditation we receive guidance from a higher power that causes us to avoid most of life's mistakes. People are made sick and miserable, mentally and physically, because they do not go into meditation every day and ask for this higher intuitive guidance from the cosmic mind that knows all, sees all and is all.

THESE TEN DYNAMIC LAWS OF MEDITATION
MAKE FOR A HEALTHY, HAPPY
LIFE EXPERIENCE

Law No. 1 Peace of Mind and Peace of Soul

When you live under cosmic laws of good, truth and love, your mind will be at peace with yourself and the world.

Go into meditation and say at least ten times:

I am at peace with myself and the world. Peace, be still; be still and know that I am God.

Let your daily Karmic actions be harmonious with the cosmic laws of the universe. Do not let yourself be swayed by emotions of greed, selfishness and hatred, for these are negative forces that release Karmic forces of mental unrest, bodily sickness and physical danger.

A man hated his business rival. He spread ugly rumors about him. Told of the man's supposed dishonesty and evil. This man never knew why he developed ulcers and high blood pressure with its attendant cardiac involvement. He was sick and miserable. He became so irritable that his wife finally left him for another man. When he came to me he cried in anguish, "What have I done that God should be punishing me?"

I pointed out the relationship between Karmic action and reaction. "The laws of cause and effect are working in your life," I told him.

"You are not being punished by God, but you are punishing yourself for the evil you have done."

Then I gave him the regimen by which he could be cured. I told him to go into daily meditation for half an hour. To forgive himself and to forgive his business rival, to bless him and release him. Then he was to pray to God for forgiveness of his Karmic evil. He was then to get in touch with his wife and beg her forgiveness and tell her he still loved her and would change.

This man followed this regimen and achieved an amazing healing, not only did his wife come back to him but his physical symptoms of bodily illness diminished, and he is on the way to achieving a balanced, happy and healthy life.

Law No. 2

For achieving good bodily health, youthful vigor and energy.

Mental action reflects in bodily and external reaction. To set into motion the Karmic pattern of mental action for good health and youthful vigor, go into a few moments meditation each day before beginning your day's activities. Hold your mind still and meditate as follows: I am now in the divine and cosmic stream of life energy and vitality. My mind is peaceful and calm. My body reflects this tranquility. The cells of my body shall sing the song of health all day. I think and act in a positive, constructive manner and my outer circumstances reflect order, harmony and balance.

Then all during the day let yourself indulge in a regimen of deep, diaphragmatic breathing, in which you inhale ten to fifteen times, exhaling the breath, and feeling that you are drinking a golden elixir of life, which spreads through your entire body, giving you life, energy, youth and health.

A woman who was having many problems in her home and business, felt constantly fatigued. She tried vitamins, and every known diet. Nothing worked, for the trouble was in her Karmic pattern of thinking and acting. She let everything annoy her. She lost her temper easily; she criticized others, she found fault with her husband and children. She had so much venom of hatred and resentment in her mind and body that it was devitalizing her and sapping all her strength.

After coming to a few of our lectures this woman learned about meditation and the laws of Karma. She began to practice them in her daily life, using the deep breathing techniques to get plenty of magnetism and electricity and life energy into her body cells. Soon she was sleeping better; she stopped taking sleeping pills; she began to smoke less and stopped drinking several cups of coffee a day to give her pep. As her mind and body built their own inner defences and when the short-circuiting of her emotional energies stopped, this woman experienced immediate benefits. It took her only two months to completely achieve a healthy, happy and serene state of mind.

Law No. 3

Meditation for solving daily problems as they arise.

When we allow problems to multiply and grow without solving them, they tend to overpower us and bring about nervous tension and illness.

To solve daily problems as they arise, go into a few moments of meditation and affirm:

> *I am now in a pool of inner and outer stillness in which all my problems are being submerged in the spiritual lake. I am serene and calm. My problems are converted into life experiences for my spiritual growth. I know that the solution to my problem is on the way and I joyously and confidently await my good.*

A doctor that I know uses this meditation at least ten to fifteen times a day. He has suffered from angina pectoris for many years and his life is so burdened with work that he can hardly get through his day. When he learned about meditation and how to clear the mental decks for action, he began to affirm this law after each patient left and before another arrived. He said that this gave him the strength to get through each day without breaking down. Even his heart condition seemed to improve after he learned how to meditate.

The law of meditation helps an actor

A star who has appeared on Broadway in many plays, is not as young as he once was, and he felt the need of some help in getting through his arduous roles. I showed him how to use this law of meditation. Just before he steps out on the stage he visualizes himself surrounded by a golden aura of life, light and energy. He affirms, "I am surrounded by infinite life, energy and vitality. I am sustained and controlled by a higher power and shall perform magnificently tonight." This man is noted for his dynamic portrayal of his characters and is more effective now than when he was younger.

Law No. 4

Meditation for overcoming worry, fear, hatred and other negative emotions.

In the study of alpha brain wave therapy in the modern scientific laboratories it has been found that people who indulge in emotions of fear, worry, hatred, selfishness, greed, jealousy and revenge, produce brain waves that actually tend to poison their bodies and make them sick.

To overcome any negative emotion, no matter its nature, go into meditation and dwell on the positive emotions.

To master worry, mentally affirm quietly for a few moments:

> *I now erase all worries from my mind. I am protected by God and I have confidence in my future destiny.*

To overcome the effects of fear, go into a few moments meditation and say the Twenty-third Psalm, and then say quietly to yourself, as you hold your mind still:

> *I now program fear out of my consciousness and in its place I put trust and confidence in the source of my life and power. I am surrounded by an aura of protection and the magic circle of God's presence is with me wherever I go.*

**A woman was saved from
danger through this method**

A woman reported to me that she was walking one night on the streets of New York, fearful and expectant of danger. Suddenly a young man darted out of the shadows and grabbed her pocket book, pulling her to the ground. She remembered a sentence I had used at one of my lectures and she said out loud, *I shall fear no evil. Thy rod and thy staff, they comfort me.* She said this with such force that the young man instantly let go of her pocketbook and ran away.

To overcome hatred, greed, selfishness and other negative emotions, go into a moment of quiet meditation and affirm to your higher mind centers; "I cannot perform any act contrary to the principles of good, love and integrity. I now put myself in attunement with cosmic mind and am filled with divine love. I forgive all those who had harmed me and I project love and understanding to every person I meet."

Law No. 5

Meditation to build spiritual values of honesty, high morality and integrity in your character.

Most misery in life comes because we build the wrong mental and spiritual values. We become material minded and forget the dynamic spiritual laws that are at the basis of all civilization.

To fortify yourself against the forces of misery, discontent and pain, go into a quiet meditation and affirm:

I now incorporate in my consciousness the highest standards and ideals that I can conceive. I know that I am created in the image and likeness of God, therefore my thoughts and actions shall be God-like, inspiring and uplifting.

Then each day practice observance of the great spiritual code known as the Ten Commandments. Follow the precepts of the Golden Rule, and the high moral laws given in the Sermon on the Mount.

A man built a great fortune through this method

A great business man named J.C. Penney built his enormous fortune of over a billion dollars through following this regimen of integrity in his dealings with the public. He told his employees to give every customer a fair deal and quality for his money. This Golden Rule principle not only made him a very rich man, but when he died at the age of ninety-five he was still working daily in his office for many hours. Our minds and bodys thrive on this regime of spiritual integrity.

Law No. 6

Each day strive to do something good and constructive for someone else. Obey your charitable impulses, give smiles and receive friendship. Give encouragement, and praise others, and they will respond with better work and more co-operation. Give love and win love and respect.

In meditation each day review the basic law of good. Meditate as follows:

God is good, therefore, I shall be good and deal with my fellow-men with honesty and goodness and I shall receive rewards and benefits that are valuable. God is love, therefore I shall conduct myself in a loving manner and be loved in return by my fellowmen.

How a Teacher Overcame
Problems Through This Law

A teacher in grammar school had tremendous problems with a racially mixed class in New York city. She was nervous and tense and her students seemed to sense fear in her aura. She learned about this meditation and when things got out of hand she went into a moment of quiet meditation and affirmed:

> *I am governed by the law of Divine Love. These students are united by bonds of love. I see perfection in them and their actions and they shall now respond to my praise and encouragement. The love of cosmic co-operation brings us all into direct communication with a superior intelligence that now prevails in this classroom.*

This meditation, repeated several times a day, caused this teacher to become so relaxed and peaceful within that it removed all her tensions, anxiety and doubt. As their teacher changed her attitude and removed the irritations and frictions from her own consciousness the students became less obstreperous and gave her less trouble than formerly.

A lawyer won more cases
through practicing this law

A young attorney who usually went into court with a belligerent attitude towards the prosecuting attorney and judge, lost most of his cases. He told me of his difficulties. I then gave him a meditation based on the teachings of Lao-Tse, and told him to remove arrogance, hostility and anger from his mind and to let his words reflect peace, calmness and a sense of victory. I then gave him this sentence from the philosophy of Lao-Tse, which he was to repeat to himself when he was in court:

A falling drop of water shall at last carve the hardest rock. Then he was to meditate as follows:

> *The gentle flow of spirit now removes the obstructing forces that stand in the way of justice. I am a channel for divine justice and no person or thing shall arouse my anger, or stay my victory.*

Opposing attorneys soon discovered they could not confuse and irritate him and began to marvel at his cool delivery. He soon gained a reputation for being level-headed and calm when others lost their poise and made serious blunders. This young man went on to become one of Southern California's most successful criminal attorneys, winning ninety percent of his cases!

Law No. 7

Adopt an optimistic cheerful nature which sees only good in everyone and everything. This attitude removes many of the nervous tensions that come when you program your mind to disaster.

Program out of your mind the negative charges that are aroused by such negative words as:

Sickness	Substitute the word	**Health**
Failure	Program the word	**Success**
Poverty	Change this to	**Riches**
Fear	Build the quality of	**Confidence**
Hate	Supplant it with	**Love**
Loss	Change this word into	**Gain**
War	Visualize permanent	**Peace**
Disaster	Affirm the reality of	**Calmness and order**
Age	See the spiritual reality	**Youth**
Impossible	Admit that all things are	**Possible**
Limitation	Affirm and see an	**Unlimited universe**

To meditate on the positive states of consciousness and remove the negative emotional charges of the above and other negative words, sit quietly in meditation and repeat the following sentences, substituting one of the positive words given above, until you have removed the negative charges from your consciousness and replaced them with the positive forces.

I now break the mold of sickness and substitute the thought of perfect health. I am mentally and physically perfect.

I program into my higher mind centers the consciousness of success, mentally, physically, financially, socially and spiritually, I am successful.

I am aware of the infinite riches in the universe, created for my use and enjoyment. I now accept abundance.

I reflect poise and confidence in my personality, my words and actions and negate all fear thoughts.

I am filled with the emotion of love and remove hate, animosity and rancor from my mind centers.

*I am aligned with great good and I gain benefits from my life
activities which enrich my life experience.*

*I am at peace with the world and with myself. No power can
move me from the safe anchor of calm and order.*

*I reflect calmness and order at the center of my being and in
the outer periphery of my life circumstances.*

*I am spiritually young and eternally joyous with the vibrant
force of youth, energy and vitality.*

*I remove the negative charge of defeat and failure and live in
the consciousness of infinite possibilities in every realm of my life
experience.*

*I meditate on the unlimited and boundless universe in which
cosmic expansion, growth, riches and abundance are mine by
divine law.*

I saw a salesman in real estate use this technique of meditation for
improving his sales until he sold more property than three of the other
salesmen combined.

A young lady who was having problems in romance had been programmed negatively all her life about love and marriage. She began to
change her meditations to include the states of consciousness repre-
sented by the words success, confidence, gain, peace and love, and she
won the heart of a young doctor and married him.

How He Programmed Himself
Into Success and Happiness

A man who had been living in the awareness of his limitations and
disaster constantly, had three accidents; he failed twice in his own
business, his marriage ended in failure. He was so programmed to
failure, disaster, loss and fear and hate, that he created his vortex of
negative happenings. I showed him the method for meditating on
success, confidence, love, gain, calmness and order, and he was soon
functioning as a happy, healthy and successful human being.

Law No. 8

Be aware of the beauty of life and accept the universe and all
therein, as being your heritage.

Most people live a life of drudgery, ugliness and mediocrity. They
fail to elevate their consciousness to heights of beauty and inspiration
and they miss out on most of the joyous experiences of life.

Each day spend a few moments on meditation, in which you once
more see the world through the eyes of a child. Affirm:

All around me there is beauty and magic. I am aware of the beauty in nature; I see sunsets and oceans, mountains and moonlit skies. I stand in awe at the wonder of the universe and I accept these cosmic miracles as being for my enjoyment and use.

Then meditate on the most memorable and beautiful scenes that you have viewed in the past. Run through your mind the most precious moments that you hold in memory. These meditations will add to your mental and spiritual enrichment and cause you to focus beauty in your consciousness.

Law No. 9

Share loving experiences with your family and friends and express love daily as a positive, constructive emotion.

To incorporate this divine emotion in your consciousness, sit for only a few moments a day and meditate as follows:

I am now in the magic circle of love. I hold in my mind loving thoughts and perform loving actions towards my fellowmen. I release all the glittering reflections from the cosmic diamond of love and love my family, humanity and God.

A young woman of twenty-five who lived a life of loneliness and misery, believed she would never attract permanent love. She had many dates but found them unsatisfactory and told me that all men seemed fickle and only wanted an emotional involvement without real love.

I gave her this meditation to use every day. I told her to change her consciousness and begin to elevate love to its true plane of divinity as the noblest and most beautiful of all emotions. She began her daily meditation on love and reported to me that she had at last met a man she thought worthy of marriage. The brain wave patterns he held regarding love were identical to hers. Like had attracted like, under the great cosmic law of magnetism, and they are on their way to a happy marriage together.

Law No. 10

Attune your mind to a glorious unison with God, the divine principle back of life and achieve a sense of oneness with cosmic power and fulfillment. This state of consciousness on which you are to meditate is known as Darshan, in Sanskrit; the finding of cosmic fulfillment or blending with the light. This is the highest stage of meditation which man may achieve.

To attain Darshan meditate as follows:

> *I am one with infinite intelligence and my mind and soul now reflect the light. I am one with infinite good and my life reflects goodness. I am one with infinite truth and my life is perfect. I am one with infinite love and my life becomes beautiful. I am one with infinite joy and know the supreme happiness that comes when one has discovered the divine romance that lasts throughout eternity.*

Review of Chapter Five

1. The invisible cosmic laws which rule the universe and how man must obey them if he wishes to be happy, healthy and prosperous.

2. The law of Karma and how it works to reward or punish us, when we work with the laws or against them.

3. How one woman violated Karmic laws and suffered untold agony of mind and body, until she corrected her Karmic pattern of destiny.

4. Meditation to be used to find peace of mind and peace of soul and overcome Karmic punishment for our sins.

5. A man who hated his business rival developed ulcers and heart trouble. He was cured only when he forgave his business rival and himself.

6. Meditation to be used to achieve good bodily health, youthful vigor and energy.

7. A woman used this meditation to overcome bodily ills and achieve energy, control of temper and peaceful relationships with those around her.

8. The meditation to use for solving daily problems and putting yourself into a state of dynamic power for overcoming life's misfortunes.

9. A doctor and an actor who use this meditation to help them increase their energy, improve their health and achieve inner tranquility.

10. Meditation to be used for overcoming fear, worry, hatred and other negative emotions.

11. How a woman who lived in fear, used this meditation to overcome a dangerous situation in her life.

12. Meditation you can use to achieve spiritual values, honesty and high morality, so you can benefit from the good forces of life and minimize the negative ones.

13. How a teacher used meditation to help her overcome problems in a racially tense classroom, and how it helped her achieve a peaceful and constructive atmosphere.

14. How to use meditation to achieve an optimistic and cheerful nature, by substituting a positive mental programming to replace the negative one.

15. How to use the meditation for love happiness and attract your true soul mate.

16. Meditation for attaining the state of Darshan, ultimate fulfillment and blending with the light of truth, love, peace, joy and good.

HOW TO INCREASE YOUR INCOME AND GROW RICH THROUGH MEDITATION — 6

The secret back of the world's greatest fortunes is the mystical power of transcendental meditation.

Such rich men as Rockefeller, Carnegie, Onassis, or Howard Hughes, built their vast financial empires because they consciously concentrated all the power of their minds on a single objective — to become rich.

Concentration is a form of intense meditation. In this chapter we shall explore the methods by which you may become successful and attain riches on all planes.

AWESOME POWERS OF THE MIND RELEASED THROUGH CONCENTRATION AND MEDITATION

When the mind is concentrated in a dynamic, radiant stream of energy towards any single objective, it helps release tremendous power that can literally perform miracles.

The brain wave rhythm found to be most effective for meditation on achieving riches and success is that which measures between fourteen and twenty-eight cycles per second, and known in the scientific laboratories as the Beta Brain Wave.

When you concentrate and meditate with intensity, it increases the rhythm of the mind and causes the brain waves to radiate electrical and magnetic properties which have a profound effect on the body and the environment.

A successful person is one who generally generates tremendous quantities of electrical brain energy.

Geniuses have a great capacity for concentration and hard work. They never seem to tire. They are fired with enthusiasm and creativity. In fact, all creativity, whether it is in writing a novel, composing a song, inventing an object, or devising a new business or industrial technique, requires hours of intense and dynamic concentration and meditation.

How a Man In Advertising Used Meditation to Get Ideas

A student of mine in New York who worked in an advertising agency for the usual salary, was so inspired when he learned about how one could use meditation to increase his income, that he began daily sessions of only half an hour each to meditate on new ideas for his company's accounts. The first week he got two marvelous new ideas that brought him substantial bonuses from his boss.

Money is important in your life and you cannot live without it. However, money is *not* success. A successful person will usually have money come to him through industry, thrift and giving something of value to the world, but a man may become rich through unscrupulous methods and still be one of the world's greatest failures.

In meditating on achieving riches, learn to balance your life. Do not love money and make it the obsession of your life, for it will tend to unbalance you, as in the case of a miser. The Bible says, "Love of money is the root of all evil."

Observe These Five Rules About Money

1. Money is a medium of exchange and in itself is not valuable.
2. True permanent values are determined by your own creative effort and what you count as important to you.
3. Money represents the frozen assets of mind and creative spirit. One idea, if it is constructive, can make you a million dollars.
4. A man from the neck down is only worth ninety-eight cents worth of chemicals; from the neck up, in the realm of creative ideas, imagination and mental power, he is worth illimitable millions.

5. Money obeys certain cosmic laws and principles, and the old adage, "Money goes to money," is true. As you magnetize the brain centers with the thought you are going to be rich and meditate daily on riches, you will begin to attract the money you hold in consciousness.

How a Businessman Used
Meditation to Grow Rich

A man who worked for a big hardware wholesale firm, learned in our lectures about how meditation could help him become rich. He began to meditate on some product which he might sell and become wealthy. Each day he sat in the stillness and projected, through meditation, the thought: I shall find some new product which I can sell exclusively, and make a fortune. A dozen times a day he thought of this idea, but he did not know what kind of a product, as there did not seem to be anything new in his field.

One day his firm sent him to Germany, as he was of German descent and spoke the language perfectly, to see about releasing some American products in that country. While he was there he kept meditating that he would discover something he could sell and make a fortune. One day, quite by accident, he found a new kind of can opener that was a great improvement over the American variety. His intuition told him this was IT! He tied up distribution rights for America, and returned to train salesmen and prepare a wide advertising campaign to sell this new product. The item sold rapidly and this man is now adding other items which he imports from Japan and Germany to his growing line. He is on the way to making a fortune.

Take These Five Simple Steps To Make
Your Mind A Money Magnet

1. Each day meditate on magnetizing your brain centers with the success theme. Study business magazines for new ideas; review old methods used in business and see how you can improve on them. Desire success and concentrate each day for at least fifteen minutes on money and how to get more.

2. Sit in meditation and go on a mental shopping spree. Visualize yourself buying the car that you desire; see yourself driving it and visiting places you want to go. Mentally buy the dream home you want to live in. Then furnish it by visualizing each room done in the style and type of furniture you want. Select the clothes, jewels, cam-

eras, tape records, record players, and other items that you always dreamed of owning, and then see yourself having and using these items.

To make this exercise in meditation on riches more real get a scrapbook and cut pictures out of magazines and newspapers of the dream home, the car, the furnishings for your home that you want, and paste them in your scrapbook. Then each day meditate for five or ten minutes on these possessions and see them as actually being yours. This stirs the creative centers of your brain with the emotion of desire and brings them into focus in your consciousness.

How a Couple Won Their Dream Home Through Meditation

While lecturing in Carnegie Hall, a young couple told me their dream. They wanted a beautiful home in the country in which they could rear their family. But the husband made a very small salary and there seemed no chance for them to ever achieve this impossible dream.

One day, while sitting in meditation, the girl got a psychic hunch to buy an Irish Sweepstakes Ticket. She told me about it and I told her I would pray with her that her ticket would win the one hundred thousand dollars.

This was a chance in a million that she would win, but when the numbers were drawn her horse came up and won the hundred thousand dollars!

Sometimes God works in a mysterious way His wonders to perform — and there may not have been any other way for this couple to buy their dream home.

I have seen instances where people have been guided to invest in a certain stock, or play a certain number in roulette and win, but this is not always advocated unless one does it only occasionally and can afford to lose.

3. Carry in your pocketbook a check made out to yourself for one million dollars. Sign it God, the Universal Banker. Put your name on it and every time you open your pocketbook and see that check you are magnetizing your brain centers with the thought that God is your source of supply and abundance. Meditate each day on this fact and see the vast cornucopia of the universe filled with treasures and pouring into your mind and your environment every good and wondrous gift that you desire.

How a Young Woman Demonstrated $5,000 Through this Meditation

A young woman who needed money to help her mother obtain an operation for cataracts, began to use this meditation to attract money. She said to herself every morning when she arose: God is my universal supply. I now magnetize my mind with the idea of infinite riches. I attract to myself the sum of $5,000 so I can help my mother regain her perfect vision.

Then this woman would sit and meditate on the check made out to herself for one million dollars. She realized that the world was filled with treasures and that $5,000 was nothing. She also meditated on her mother's perfect vision, realizing that no amount of money could be set as a value for that priceless gift of sight.

After two weeks of this type of meditation the mother received a letter from a brother who had gone to Australia twenty years before and had become estranged from the family. He had struck it rich with an opal mine and sent a check for exactly $5,000 to his sister!

4. Occasionally put yourself into the atmosphere of wealth and opulence. Go to a good restaurant occasionally and observe how rich people live. Sit in a hotel lobby like the Waldorf Astoria in New York, and absorb the atmosphere of opulence and abundance. Visit the stock market in your city and buy the Wall Street Journal and read about how vast fortunes are made and lost. Buy or take books from the public library on the lives of Morgan, Rockefeller, Onassis, Paul Getty, Howard Hughes and other multimillionaires. Learn their methods, their thoughts, their philosophies and then try to emulate some of their principles and apply them to your own life.

How a Young Man Used This Method to Become a Success

A young man from Greece Named Chris P. came into our lecture work in New York city and applied these principles to his life. He worked as a waiter in a Greek restaurant but he was not satisfied with his slow progress. He sat in daily meditation to ask for guidance on how to be more successful. He got a hunch to apply for a job in a stock brokerage office in Manhattan so he could be in the atmosphere of wealth. His work was to deliver stocks and other papers between brokerage offices. In this way he had access to confidential papers which often gave inside information on stocks that were good investments.

Chris did not have any cash to invest but he knew the owner of the Greek restaurant where he had worked and he impressed him with the knowledge he had gained about stocks. One certain stock, American Industries, was very low; Chris saw inside information that this stock would go up, so he urged his former boss to invest in it and promise to give Chris part of his earnings. The boss took the information, and bought one thousand shares of the stock and when it began to go up, Chris told him when to sell it and they made thousands of dollars on their investment! From that time on Chris had money with which to play the market and, still keeping his job as a messenger, he kept getting tips that made him the sum of $20,000 within three years time!

5. When you meditate on success and money do not simply ask for money, but have some reason why you want money. This is called Cosmic Motivation and gives an added impetus to your mind to make a fortune for some specific purpose.

There are three cosmic motivators on which you should meditate each day:

A desire to help yourself or your family.

A desire to create beauty for the world.

A desire to educate, uplift, inspire and improve the world to higher levels of civilization.

Almost all great fortunes have been built through one or all of these cosmic motivators.

Sit in meditation each day and put in the forefront of your mind one or more of these cosmic motivators. Affirm to yourself: I am now inspired to creative action and the building of a fortune for the purpose of helping my family, of creating beauty for the world, and to uplift and improve the standards of humanity, to abolish war, to create peace and otherwise bring God's blessings to the world.

How a Woman Founded a Music School For Orphans

A woman in our lecture group was a musician but had married early and given up her career. She had no children of her own but loved them and began to work with orphans. One day in meditation she got the inspiring idea to found a music school and give scholarships to orphans who were talented musically. She gave a concert and announced her plans. She raised the sum of $7,000 with pledges for more to help her found the school. In the years past she has helped thousands of orphans obtain a musical education without charge and has kept herself occupied and happy through the years.

Follow This Regimen to Increase Your Income and Grow Rich

1. Take a Mental Inventory of The Universal Treasures.

To start your mind on the pathway to riches and abundance, on all planes, first take a mental inventory of the universal treasures that exist for you to use and enjoy.

God has created not one, but thousands of varieties of trees, plants, fruits and vegetables to nourish mankind and provide shelter for his family.

Every time you see a growing tree meditate on the fact that this is your future dream home. There is enough uncut lumber in one forest in Russia alone to build and furnish a home the size of the White House in Washington, D.C. for every family in the entire world!

See how the earth and oceans teem with treasures. There is coal, steel, oil, copper and uranium to furnish mankind with treasures for generations to come. And now, in the realm of atomic power, new forms of power will be introduced to humanity which, so science says, will cause each person to fly with his own little personal atomic power station, and go through the air to any place on the face of the earth with ease! Scientists are also predicting that man will harness cosmic magnetism in his flying machines and be able to fly at the incredible speed of two hundred and fifty thousand miles per hour!

How a Businessman Invoked These Laws of Meditation and Became Enormously Successful

William S. was a businessman in Southern California who invoked these laws of meditation and became enormously successful and rich.

When Mr. S. came into our classes and learned how to meditate, he was dabbling in many different things trying to make money. He complained to me, "Here I am at forty-five years of age, with a wife and two grown sons, and I have been a colossal failure all my life!"

I changed his thinking and told him to think of himself not as a failure, but a delayed success. I told him how to change his thinking and in classes he and his wife learned how to go into meditation and use this power to open the centers of consciousness for wealth.

He began his daily meditation sessions with this statement: *I am aware that the world is teeming with riches and abundance. I now claim my share of the world's wealth.*

Then he was to mentally ask for higher guidance to the source of his riches. His conscious mind had tried everything and failed. I told him to no longer trust such an unreliable source for his future guidance. I told him to open higher psychic centers through meditation and then sit in stillness at least a half an hour a day, waiting for guidance to come through. He took into his meditation with him a piece of paper on which he had written:

> I desire financial security for my family.
>
> I ask for the sum of $50,000 or more so I can have financial freedom in the future.
>
> I have faith in the power of my higher mind to manifest anything I desire.
>
> I give thanks for my supply and abundance and confidently await results.

After several days of meditation, while he was walking one day on the outskirts of the town he happened to live, which was in California, he noticed the wide expanses of land that stretched away as far as the eye could see. He mentally claimed this land, and his mind began to expand to see himself as owning it and subdividing it for homes. But how? He didn't have more than five hundred dollars in the bank and his future was most insecure. He continued meditating and one day he was guided to read a book on real estate development in which he learned about something called Option Buying. He had never heard of such a thing, but he studied the principles given in the book and found out how it worked. He was now convinced that his higher mind was trying to tell him something about how he could become rich.

He consulted an attorney and formed a corporation for land development. Without a penny he began to buy up land in the outskirts of the city, and on the option principle he began to put big ads in Los Angeles papers telling about the wholesome air and beautiful environment, and offering lots to city people who were anxious to get away from the confusion and pollution of a big city.

He conducted tours with a bus to his development, and people began to buy lots and acreage. With this money he was able to pay down payments on his land when the options came due, and soon he had four salesmen working for him and a new city sprouting up before his very eyes!

2. If you have not had any luck in using your conscious mind to attract success and riches, try meditation and contact the higher, subconscious mind for this purpose. Sit in meditation for fifteen minutes a day and give your subconscious mind the instructions that you want it to obey. You can use the following meditation for this purpose:

"I now call upon my subconscious mind to guide me automatically to obtaining wealth. I instruct it to give me ideas at night while I sleep, and during the day, on how to increase my income and become more successful. I desire the sum of $1,000 within two months time from unexpected sources."

A man in the manufacturing business uses this technique of meditation to bring him new ideas for selling his products. He meditates just before going to sleep and asks for guidance. He invariably receives some new ideas while sleeping, and awakens to jot them down. He is always amazed when he reads them over the next day. He marvels that his conscious mind can never think as clearly when he is awake.

3. Program your higher mind with the positive idea that riches are all about you and that it is easy to become successful and rich. Look at every building and let it remind you of infinite lumber, cement and building materials that exist in the world. Look at clothing in the windows of shops and program your mind that everything you need to wear in the future is already being produced somewhere in the world. Every time you eat a meal or see food in a restaurant, remind your higher mind that your nourishment has already been arranged for all time to come and that you will be lacking in nothing to nourish your body perfectly. When you look at gold and silver and jewelry in shop windows tell yourself: The storehouse of cosmic riches is now open and pours forth its abundance for my use and enjoyment.

4. Whenever you ride in a bus, taxi or subway affirm: I now possess the greatest limousine in the world and it is chauffeured for me and efficiently meets my needs. Whenever you walk in a park, remind yourself: This is my free estate and I now claim it. I am richer than Rockefeller.

5. Each time you turn on your television or radio set meditate on this reality: This program has been especially prepared for me by skilled artists and workmen. I now accept a million dollar entertain-

ment from a billion dollar industry and I am enriched, entertained and educated by this program.

6. Each time you walk into an art gallery, a public library or a museum silently affirm your riches as follows: I accept these billions of dollars worth of treasures as mine. I now enjoy this heritage of the thousands of creative minds that have labored to bring me beauty, inspiration, education and culture. I am blessed and enriched by this knowledge.

7. Every time you look at some magnificent scene in nature and enjoy a sunrise or sunset, or a vista of the ocean stretching out to the distant horizon, or the starlit sky, with its full moon, stop for a moment and remind yourself in quiet meditation of how truly rich you are and how you have inherited the universe and all therein: Father, I thank thee for all these blessings of natural beauty. I marvel at the golden sun. I absorb the infinite beauty of stars and moon and the silvery splendor spread upon the earth's seas for my enjoyment. I absorb the wonder of cerulean blue skies, oceans reaching out to infinity and the cosmic wonder of all created things which have been brought forth for my delectation and use.

Review of Points in Chapter Six

1. The secret power back of all the world's great fortunes is the mystical power of transcendental meditation.

2. Concentration and meditation when used together release awesome powers of the mind and cause the brain waves to work in the Beta cycle of creativity and success.

3. How a man in advertising used meditation to receive new ideas for his work that brought him substantial bonuses.

4. How a miser uses the powers of concentration and meditation to build a fortune, but because he loves money, it usually destroys him.

5. The five rules about money: It is a medium of exchange and has no value in itself — true permanent values are determined by your creative effort. Money represents the frozen assets of your creative spirit, from the neck up you are worth millions in the realm of ideas. Money goes to money and you can magnetize your brain centers with riches.

6. How a man opened new sources of income when he sat in daily meditation and found a new product in Germany which brought him great success.

7. How to magnetize your brain centers with the success theme and build riches in consciousness first before they come to focus in the material realm.

8. How to go on a mental shopping spree and see yourself buying a car, owning a dream home, adorning yourself with fine clothing, valuable jewels and other items yo˙ desire.

9. How a couple won their dream home by using meditatior and being guided to buy a Sweepstakes ticket which wor them $100,000.

10. How one young woman needed help to give her mother an eye operation and projected through meditation the sum of $5,000. Within two weeks a rich uncle in Australia sent her a check for that exact amount!

11. How to create an atmosphere of wealth and opulence by visiting expensive hotels. the stock market, fine restaurants, until you can duplicate the power to bring you into these environments as a wealthy person.

12. How a young Greek, Chris P. started working as a waiter in a restaurant, until he learned of the mystical power of meditation. He obtained work in a stock brokerage office, got tips on stocks and soon had built a fortune of $20,000.

13. The three cosmic motivators that you can meditate on to bring you a fortune.

14. How a woman founded a school for orphans to study music and soon raised $7,000 to carry on her dedicated work.

15. How a businessman invoked these laws of meditation and at forty-five years of age got the idea to do a big subdivision in land, creating a new town and making a fortune.

16. How to program your higher mind with the positive idea that riches and abundance are all about you in the realm of nature and how to attract your abundance and riches.

THE FOUR STAGES OF MYSTIC MEDITATION TO ACHIEVE PSYCHIC AND CLAIRVOYANT PERCEPTION

7

Every person is born with psychic and clairvoyant powers. When you were created you possessed a mysterious psychic communication with your mother's brain and body which was able to tell your growing body what chemicals you needed to form a perfect child in nine months time.

There are invisible lines of psychic communication between all living things in the universe. When you know how to use this power you will be intuitively guided to your right destiny in life.

In this chapter we shall learn how to re-discover this psychic power which you may have lost through the years.

Psychic power expresses itself in many forms. It is known as intuition, clairvoyance, clairaudience, precognition, mental telepathy, telekinesis, cosmic perception and spiritism. The techniques for developing all these various forms of psychism are the same. Mystic meditation is the means by which you may reach into the higher psychic centers of consciousness and channel the tremendous forces that await your joyous discovery.

SCIENTIST PROVES
EVEN PLANTS ARE PERCEPTIVE

A scientist recently performed amazing experiments with the electro-encephalograph, in which he proved that even plants possess cosmic and psychic perception and are aware of things going on in their environment.

When the scientist approached the plant with a knife and said, "I am going to cut off your leaves." The plant released distress and alarm signals on the measuring machine, showing that it not only heard but understood the spoken threat to its safety.

Then the scientist did the same thing with fire, threatening to burn the plant and once again it reacted with alarm signals. Then the scientist changed his tactics and merely thought the words "I am going to cut off your leaves." The plant instantly reacted with alarm, showing that it was aware not only of the spoken threat but also of the thoughts directed to it! This proved conclusively that all living things are in psychic communication with each other and with some higher cosmic intelligence that makes us all inter-related.

However, the most significant proof that plants are capable of receiving the transmission of thoughts, came about quite accidentally. When the scientist's wife put live shrimp into boiling water, the plant sent out the same distress signals that it had emitted when its own safety was threatened! This proved that it had perception and awareness of what was going on in its environment.

WHY SOME PEOPLE HAVE A GREEN THUMB

This is why some people, who love plants and all growing things have the proverbial green thumb and things grow under the impetus of their love better than they do for others.

A minister tried an experiment with praying over seed and blessing it. This seed multiplied and grew better and yielded a bigger crop than seed which was not prayed over! Then when some seed that had been planted was cursed, the seed shriveled and died!

Scientists now know that this principle of blessing or cursing may be indulged by people and they will thrive and flourish, be healthy, prosperous and successful, when the right meditations are released, and when the wrong meditations are indulged, the human brain and body react in a negative way and develop all kinds of limitations, illnesses and symptoms of distress and failure.

HOW A WOMAN CURSED HERSELF
AND HER ENVIRONMENT
TO HER DISADVANTAGE

An example of how this power works negatively to destroy, was that of a woman who was sick from a variety of illnesses. She could find no reason for her illness physically, but the symptoms were very real. She suffered from rapid heart; her blood pressure fluctuated, sometimes it was very high and sometimes very low. She felt constantly tired and depressed and had no joy in living.

After talking to this woman for half an hour I found the cause of her strange symptoms. She had been married ten years when she discovered that her husband was having an affair with another woman. Her first reaction was one of shock and hatred. She could never forgive her husband and she would not divorce him for it was against her religion to do so. She lived for five years in a home that was filled with bitterness and hate. She began developing strange symptoms within a few months time and at times she was in such pain and agony that she had seriously considered killing herself.

It was at this stage that I met her. She sought me out in desperation, for as she told me, she had reached the end of the rope and did not know what to do or where to go.

I urged this woman to go into daily periods of meditation and ask for guidance from her higher psychic centers. She was so confused that there was no contact with this higher power. Then she was to forgive her husband, and if possible, to try to rebuild the life they had known formerly. At first this woman received no guidance while she sat in meditation. But gradually, as she stopped hating her husband and began to forgive him, her mind cleared up and one day in meditation she felt a sudden release within her mind and body. She knew that by forgiving her husband she also forgave herself and from that moment on, her relationship with her husband changed. They gradually adjusted their differences and went on to a much happier marriage than formerly. Her health problems miraculously disappeared within six weeks time!

How to Achieve the Four Stages of Mystic
Meditation for Psychic and Clairvoyant Perception

1. In your first stage of meditation sit quietly for a few moments and put yourself into what is known as the Alpha state. This is the

state where your brain rhythms are slowed down to between eight to twelve cycles per second. In this state of consciousness you will contemplate on the mind and its many facets

Be aware that you possess a higher mind than your conscious mind As you hold your mind still, visualize the lake and see its surface calm and still. As you comtemplate on mind be aware every time a disturbing or negative thought rises to the surface of consciousness. When you have achieved absolute stillness of your conscious mind, your higher psychic faculties will be opened and will make their revelations to your consciousness.

2. When you have achieved this absolute stillness of the Alpha brain wave state, you may ask your higher psychic centers various questions and await the answers;

> What work should I do?
> Whom should I marry?
> Where can I get the $1,000 I need?
> Should I trust this man?
> What business should I go in?
> Where should I live?

You may not recieve an immediate answer while sitting in meditation, so go about your regular activities and the answer may come about in the most unexpected way.

How a Man Used This Technique and Received Business Guidance

A man I once knew had a tremendous business problem and he did not know what to do. He learned of this technique of meditating, and each day for a few moments, he went into the Alpha state and asked his higher psychic centers what he should do.

Within three days time this man was guided to write a letter to someone in another state, who was in the same business. This man suggested a merger of their two companies, and this solved all the problems that had been puzzling him. No doubt his higher mind sent through the instructions to write that letter that solved his problem.

How a Girl Was Warned About Her Fiance

A girl had been going with a young man who wanted to marry her. He was seemingly respectable, had a good job, and the girl felt she was very much in love with him. However, she felt a vague sense of unease as the date for their wedding approached. She learned about psychic perception from me and sat in meditation for a week or so, and kept getting this psychic feeling that something was wrong. One day, quite by accident, she was sitting in a beauty parlor having her hair done, when she heard two women talking. She heard the name of her boy friend, and out of curiosity she listened. She was shocked when she heard one of the women say that her fiance was being sued by an unmarried girl who claimed he was the father of her child! She rushed home and confronted the young man and he admitted that he had lied to her and confessed that the story was true!

If this girl had not sat in meditation and contacted her higher mind it is unlikely she would have discovered the truth about her intended husband. She broke the engagement and was grateful she had found out in time.

3. *Telepathic communication* with others is now scientifically proved to be possible. In a famous medical college a woman psychologist conducted an experiment with thirty-eight students. She had them concentrate on sending thought forms telepathically to a group of thirty-eight soldiers stationed near Denver, Colorado. Fifty percent of these experiments proved successful. When the sender and receiver were in tune with each other, it was found that their brain waves became identical!

Twins were used in another experiment and they had telepathic communication with each other at a distance of over three hundred miles. At the exact moment of attunement with each other their brain waves became identical and their hearts beat as one!

When you wish to project your thoughts to the mind of another person, sit in quiet meditation. Remove all worries and anxieties from your mind. Relax your mind and body by saying the mystic mantra from Tibet: *Ohm mane padme ohm.* Do this ten to fifteen times, breathing deeply as you do so. The breath furnishes the electrical and magnetic motive power for transmission or reception of thought.

Hold the face of the person in the forefront of your mind as you project your thought. Then say your words to yourself or aloud. "John I want you to get in touch with me. It is important that you call me."

Or if it is a form of action that you wish the person to take, give the mental command repeating it several times in a firm, quiet voice, feeling emotionally that you are speaking direct to the person.

How a Businessman Detected
Fraud through This Method

A man who had come to some of my classes on mental telepathy in New York city felt that his business partner was committing fraud and keeping some of the income. Instead of confronting him in person he employed mental telepathy to reach his business partner's mind. He sat in meditation a few moments each night before going to sleep. He talked to his business partner saying, "Harry, I know you are keeping out money from our accounts. I insist that you stop this practice and that you will voluntarily tell me about your thefts and make restitution."

In exactly one week his business partner came into his home and told him he wanted to talk to him. They sat in the library and the man confessed all his thefts. He begged forgiveness, promised restitution, and offered to sell his share of the business to his partner! He had been losing heavily in gambling and had stolen the money to cover his gambling losses.

4. To receive the thoughts of others go into the stillness and meditate on the person you wish to be in communication with. This type of meditation can be indulged any time of the day or night, and it does not matter if the person is thousands of miles away.

As you hold the person's face in mind, feel the emotions that you would normally feel if you were with the person.

Then sit quietly and let thoughts pour into your mind. When you are psychically attuned to the person you will have a feeling of oneness, and your mind will feel it is being given thoughts from an outer source.

A woman was sitting thinking about a friend she had not seen for some months. She was wondering where she was and what she was doing. Within five minutes her phone rang and she was startled to hear her friend's voice. She said, "I got back into town yesterday and I just felt a hunch to call you now. You must have been thinking about me!"

5. To participate in the psychic phenomena known as *clairvoyance* and *clairaudience*, you go into the stillness and hold your mind perfectly calm and still. Then let pictures pass through your mind, without any conscious direction or control on your part. Many times you will feel that you are merely using your imagination, but very often you are

tuning in on actual clairvoyant images that have been released by someone's mind.

CLAIRVOYANT WARNINGS OF DANGER

A woman had a very disturbing clairvoyant vision that came to her at night while she slept. She saw an automobile turning over and bursting into flames. She could not go back to sleep and the next morning she told her husband of what she had seen. Two days later she received word that her brother was killed in a motor accident in which his car had turned over in Italy and he had burned to death!

If you practice the reception of clairvoyant images you may get warnings of danger that you can avoid. You may also receive ideas that will help you financially or some idea for an invention, a song, a story or a painting may come through clairvoyantly which can make you a great deal of money.

CLAIRVOYANT AUTHORS

I know an author who gets all his stories clairvoyantly. He sits in meditation and lets his mind become a blank. Then on the screen of his mind he projects all the characters that he uses in his story. Even the dialogue and description come through perfectly.

Robert Louis Stevenson claimed that he received all his stories clairvoyantly. He was bedridden for years, and he said that his characters paraded before his mind's eye, and performed their actions and spoke their words perfectly. All he did was to record these clairvoyant images on paper.

6. To receive predictions of your future, known as precognition, sit in meditation and ask for your higher, psychic mind to unfold the design of your future destiny. As everything you will ever do is inscribed on the akashic record of your spiritual self, these events and incidents will unravel before your psychic gaze very much like pictures that are projected by a motion picture projector on a screen.

Start this process of precognition by deliberately holding certain scenes in your mind and then asking this higher psychic mind to reveal something to you about the events which will occur.

Sit in stillness and meditate on the reality back of life. See your life unfolding progressively to its ultimate and logical conclusion. Your soul will know of its mystical purpose for living and reveal to you the golden tapestry of dreams which can make up your glorious future destiny.

I remember once rowing on a shallow lake in upstate New York. As the boat idled near shore, I looked down into the waters and saw many little black beetles swimming in the mud at the bottom of the lake. Finally one of them crawled up the oar and emerged from the water. It sat there for some time until it was thoroughly dry. Then I observed a miracle occuring before my very eyes. The hard shell of the beetle split up the back and from the shell there emerged a dragonfly with irridescent wings and seventeen hundred eyes! In a few moments this miraculous creature flew away into the sunshine and a puff of wind blew the black empty shell back into the water. It sank to the bottom of the stream and the little crawling creatures in the mud swam around it curiously, never realizing that they were part of a miracle which would one day bring about their metamorphisis from crawling creatures in the mud to winged miracles able to fly!

Your soul has visions and perceptions denied to your mortal mind. Sit in meditation daily and seek out the guidance of your higher mind. The soul is the vehicle for the transmission of higher impulses and only in meditation and stillness can you be aware of the divine voice that speaks to man in the stillness of his own immortal soul.

Review of Chapter Seven

1. You were born with psychic and clairvoyant powers, and can receive communication from a higher cosmic mind that knows your future destiny.

2. Scientific proof that growing plants are aware of what is happening in their environment and possess a form of psychic communication with mankind.

3. A woman cursed her life by using psychic power in a negative manner. She became sick until she learned how to listen to her higher psychic mind, which guided her to her right course of action.

4. How you can go into meditation and put yourself into the Alpha state where you may receive or send telepathic thought forms.

5. How a man used this power to receive guidance in his business that brought him great success.

6. A young woman used psychic guidance to learn secrets about her fiance's infidelity, which proved to be correct.

7. How to sit in meditation and use your mind as a sending station, to send thoughts to the minds of others.

8. A businessman detected fraud in his partner through meditation and psychic unfoldment.

9. How to receive the thoughts of others while you sit in psychic meditation and know secrets about the lives of others.

10. How you can open your psychic centers to receive clairvoyant and clairaudient impressions from the minds of others and from the cosmic mind that knows all secrets.

11. A woman saw an automobile accident in a clairvoyant vision, and two days later she received word her brother had been killed in a car crash.

12. How to receive precognition and predictions about future events in your life through meditation

HOW TO USE THE DREAMLESS SLEEP MEDITATION TO OVERCOME LIFE'S DAILY PROBLEMS

8

From ancient India there comes to us a powerful state of meditation called Sushupti — the dreamless sleep. In this state of meditation you can rise above sickness and pain, you can solve problems and not experience worry and anxiety from them. You can literally become a super-being with amazing powers of the mind and body.

Yogis who practice this Sushupti meditation are able to walk over red hot coals and experience no pain. They can stop the flow of blood at will; they can regulate their heartbeat and blood pressure. They are able to go without food or water for several days. They can be buried alive and are able to suspend their breathing and other body functions.

How You Can Use Sushupti Meditation While Awake

As taught in the Far East, the state of meditation known as Sushupti can be used when you are wide awake. You can consciously will yourself into this state of meditation and achieve a condition akin to self-hypnosis, in which you will have keen perception and tap higher powers of the mind which you could never do in ordinary states of consciousness.

YOU MAY USE SUSHUPTI
TO ESCAPE LIFE'S PAIN

This meditation of Sushupti may be used to escape pain, to overcome disturbing problems and to immunize you from the agony of heartbreak, loneliness, sickness and suffering of all kinds.

A woman I once knew, who had studied this branch of Oriental philosophy with me, was in a situation in her life where she went through painful agony for weeks and she was able to rise above the suffering by daily going into the meditation of Sushupti. Her little 6-year-old daughter was left alone in the house for a short time, and played with matches. When the mother returned to the house she found her daughter lying in the living room, her clothing completely burned off her body. The child was unconscious and badly burned over two-thirds of her body.

At the hospital doctors despaired of saving the little girl's life. Her mother prayed frantically for a miracle, then she remembered about the meditation for Sushupti and she knew that if she was to keep from going crazy with grief, she must do something fast. She went into Sushupti and put her mind out of reach of the pain and despair she was experiencing. A great calm settled over her and for days, her husband later told her, she walked around doing everything automatically and instinctively, but like a sleep walker. She never again had a sense of violent grief or guilt or pain. She released the little girl to God's loving care and from that moment on she was serene and calm. Fortunately, after many weeks in the hospital, the little girl recovered completely.

How to Go Into the Dreamless
Sleep Meditation

1. When you go into the meditation known as Sushupti, prepare yourself as though you were going into a little sleep. Breathe deeply and rhythmically, counting four as you inhale, then hold the breath to the count of four, and then release the breath. The indrawn breath can be through the nose, and the exhaled breath can be through the mouth.

2. With your eyes closed visualize the spiritual mountain top in the distance. You have seen pictures of Mt. Everest or Fujiyama, with their snow-capped peaks. Try to form this mental image of a

mountain and then mentally ascend up that mountain by gradual stages. As you begin your climb up from the lowlands of pain, sickness, mortal suffering, war, and death, meditate as follows:

I now ascend the spiritual mountain top, rising above the lowlands of mortal mind suffering and pain. I aspire now to the limitless celestial realms where I can expand my consciousness to encompass eternity. No life experience can now hold my aspiring soul. I rise above all problems and all physical obstructions, into the spiritual stratosphere where I find the true reality back of life. All my earth experiences now become as dreams, fading away into their native nothingness, and I enter into the state of Sushupti, the eternal Dream where I partake of God's consciousness of immortality. I am free of suffering. I am free of pain. I am free of earthly loss and bereavement. I know only eternal joy and ecstasy as I now achieve the spiritual mountain top and find God's dwelling place.

3. To achieve the state of Sushupti meditation for controlling the body and its functions, go into quiet meditation, visualizing the spiritual mountain top. Then mentally force your mind to any part of the body that you wish to control. If you have been told by your doctor that you have a heart condition, direct the life force to the heart with the following meditation and command: I now direct my psychic energy and life force to my heart. It is now being regulated to beat at approximately seventy-two beats per minute. I direct this life force to heal my heart and to bring my blood pressure to normal. I remove all thoughts of fear and anxiety from my mind and I am in perfect health.

4. To overcome *insomnia* and go to sleep immediately use the meditation of Sushupti as follows: Lie in your bed in a perfectly relaxed state and breathe ten or fifteen times, deeply and exhaling the breath as though you are sighing. Gently close your eyes and meditate as follows: I now enter the dreamless sleep of Sushupti. My mind is peaceful and still. I now ascend the spiritual mountain top. I am relaxed and feel a deep sense of peace and tranquility. I am one with all the cosmic forces of peace, beauty, love and joy. I rise now and ascend to the supernal heights as my body becomes lighter and I float away, as though on a cloud. Peace, peace, peace.

5. To solve problems and daily worries, go into the state of meditation known as Sushupti as follows. Sit quietly in a chair, or lie on your bed. Close your eyes and do the deep breathing ten or fifteen

times. Then make your body rigid for a few seconds, and then relax your body. Do this four or five times, until you are relaxed from head to toe.

Then give yourself the following meditation, as you keep your eyes closed: I am now withdrawing my sense perceptions from the outer world of problems and turmoil. I am now within my own cathedral of the soul, where my senses are lulled into a state of perpetual peace. Through the stained glass windows of my soul I now meditate on the golden glow of God's eternal presence. My mind and body are now suffused with the light of peace, infinite love and truth. I rise now to the spiritual mountain top, leaving the shadow-filled lowlands of mortal mind despair far behind me.

Then have a feeling of rising, as though going up in an airplane, until you feel a sense of complete detachment from the world and its problems.

6. To release creative power and enhance your imagination for some special inspiration, you can use the meditation of Sushupti. Many artists paint better because they use this meditation. Writers and poets go into Sushupti when they want inspiration to create magnificent masterpieces. Inventors have used this technique for meditation when they desired some special knowledge to invent some object. This meditation is good for anyone who wants to release his powers of imagination for creative work. A businessman I once knew often did this Sushupti meditation a few moments several times a day when he wanted to have new ideas to improve his business. A famous actress I know in Hollywood, learned of this meditation, and just before stepping before the cameras she goes into a five minute meditation of Sushupti, in which she achieves a state of suspension of her conscious mind and she says she literally becomes the character she meditates on.

Sit in meditation for special creative powers and quietly treat your higher mind centers with this meditation: I now suspend my conscious mind and open my creative centers of vision and imagination. I am now a channel for the reception of new and wonderful ideas for my work. I am in the center of a creative whirlpool and my imagination is now stimulated to create something of great and enduring beauty for the world.

7. You can use the meditation of Sushupti to release what the

mystics of India call the Celestial Pranic Fire within your brain and body.

This is helpful for achieving absolute mastery of your brain and body. It is used to control the nervous energy of the body. It is helpful for removing obstacles and disturbing elements from your environment. It can be used to create a dynamic personality of magnetism, poise, charm and power.

Sit in meditation and breathe deeply ten or fifteen times. Hold the breath to a count of four. When you breathe in visualize the breath or pranic life force flowing down the left side of the spinal column. Then hold the breath to the count of four and then release the breath, visualizing the breath like a golden ball of fire rising up the right side of the spinal column. When it reaches the base of the brain, see this ball of golden flame bursting like a fireworks display and showering the entire brain area with its celestial flame.

A CONCERT PIANIST USES
SUSHUPTI TO ENCHANT AUDIENCES

I know a famous concert pianist who has appeared in Carnegie Hall many times, who uses this state of Sushupti to arouse his creative brain centers with such power that he is able to hold his audiences spellbound throughout his performance. He meditates for ten minutes before he faces his audience and projects the creative golden flame to his brain centers. He says that this meditation relaxes him and he feels that the earthbound, negative forces that have been accumulating in his brain, are completely burned away, leaving the pure, celestial inspiration of heavenly music within his mind and soul.

A Review of Chapter Eight

1. The Meditation from India known as Sushupti and how the dreamless sleep helps you overcome sickness and solve all problems.

2. The mysterious Delta brainwave which scientists discovered, that gives one clairvoyant dreams, astral flights, and strange dreams, and how Sushupti takes one into Delta.

3. How this power works in the realm of nature through hibernation for the polar bear, and in the caterpillar when it goes into the dreamless sleep of Sushupti to become a golden-winged butterfly.

4. You can use Sushupti to escape life's pain, to overcome problems and immunize yourself from the agony of loneliness, heartache and suffering.

5. How a woman used Sushupti meditation when her little girl was burned in a near-fatal accident. She was able to withdraw her mind from the agony and suffering through Sushupti.

6. How to ascend the spiritual mountain top in the Sushupti meditation and rise into the eternal dream where there are no problems, pain, sickness or suffering.

7. How to go into Sushupti meditation to control the body's functions, regulate the heart and blood pressure.

8. How to use Sushupti to overcome insomnia and instantly go to sleep at night, without the aid of sleeping pills.

9. How to use the meditation of Sushupti to overcome daily problems, worries and anxieties and find eternal peace.

10. How to release creative power and imagination through Sushupti to do great creative work. A famous actress in Hollywood uses this meditation just before going in front of the cameras.

11. How to release the mystical celestial pranic fire within your brain and body through the meditation of Sushupti.

12. A concert pianist uses this meditation when he performs and holds his audiences spellbound.

13. How to attain the highest spiritual purity and state of perfection through going into the meditation of Sushupti.

HOW TO DEVELOP
SUPERIOR MENTAL POWERS
AND ACHIEVE MASTERY ── 9
OF LIFE THROUGH
MEDITATION

In the mystic lands of the Far East, where Meditation originated, anyone who had conquered himself and mastered life, was called a Master. These great Masters or Gurus, were able to completely control the power of the mind and body. They could perform miracles of healing; they had boundless energy; they delayed the erosions of age and many of them achieved life spans of one hundred and twenty years of age and more.

In this chapter we shall learn how to use the power of transcendental meditation to develop superior mental powers and achieve mastery of life.

THE FOUR SACRED MEDITATIONS

There are four sacred meditations which you can use that bring what is known as Absorption with the Light. The Light being Cosmic Spirit, or what we in our Western world call God. This cosmic mind that radiates throughout time and space can only be contacted when your own conscious mind is still. Then you may reach through the cloudbanks of confusion and misinformation, and contact the cosmic mind which is the repository of all knowledge and all power.

The Cosmic Memory bank can be tapped by your own higher psychic mind centers. You can use this knowledge to shape any world you choose.

For centuries man was earthbound because he did not expand his consciousness to these higher planes. A little over a hundred years ago there were no automobiles, no airplanes, television, telephones, motion pictures, or electric lights. When man grew wings of the soul he tapped the invisible cosmic memory bank and received the divine inspiration to create greatness.

First Sacred Meditation

Sit in the stillness and go into the first Absorption. This is known as the meditation of mind on Mind, and is for the purpose of awakening the higher mind centers to bring your mind into contact with the cosmic mind that knows all things.

Say the sacred Mantra from Tibet ten times aloud: *Ohm mane padme ohm.* Breathe deeply before you say each Mantra, and after you say the Ohm, gently close your lips, holding the ohm for a few seconds, before saying the mane padme ohm. Let the vibrations rise into the head region. This gives a gentle massage to the head and helps open the higher centers, known as Chakras, where the intuitive mind power resides.

Now meditate on your conscious mind. Be aware of memory, imagination, visualization, concentration, and all attributes of mind.

Repeat the following meditation to yourself:

I am now aware of Mind in all its aspects. My conscious mind now makes choices of the thoughts I shall think. I am aware of memory and imagination. I now tap the hidden knowledge that is within the cosmic memory bank. My mind is now attuned to the higher cosmic mind that knows all, sees all and is all things. I release the power of my imagination. I am in the light of creative mind power. I concentrate all the power of my mind on memory retention, on mental images of the world I wish to create. I live in the mental world of my own choice. I project thought forms of health, and my body responds with vitality and energy. I project thought forms of success and riches, and I am guided to the more abundant life. I project thought forms of superior mental power and I become creative.

Science calls this meditation
"Theta" state

In the scientific laboratories, it has now been found that when a person goes into this form of meditation and absorption with the light, it reduces the brain waves to a slow rhythm of from four to seven cycles per second. This is the state of meditation used by geniuses who slowly evolve their creative patterns and ideas for art, music, literature, inventions and discoveries of new ideas.

How a College Student Increased
His Grades Through Theta

Through this Theta state of meditation a college student who was getting consistently low grades, was able to improve his grades and passed at the head of his class! He had no memory retention until he learned how to slow down the brain rhythm and achieve the First Absorption in Mystic Meditation.

To attain absolute power in concentration, and achieve the Theta state of meditation, go back in your memory to the earliest recollections you have of your childhood. As you slow down the stream-of-consciousness to the Theta state, you focus the powers of the mind specifically on one thing at a time. Memory retention utilizes this same principle. As you slow down your thought processes and fix mental images in your mind by concentration on them, they will leave deep imprints on the convolutions of your brain and you will have total recall of everything you see, hear, read, or think.

How a Man Used This Meditation
to Become a Supersalesman

A man I once knew who was a salesman of household appliances, lacked concentration and could never close a sale. He came into a study of these Theta principles and began to practice the first absorption. He used the Theta Meditation and affirmed that his mind was superior, that he would be persuasive and forceful in his presentation of the sales points he wanted to make. Each time before he approached a customer he would go into the Theta state and meditate as follows: "I now slow down my conscious mind. I am in the Theta meditation. I shall speak slowly and convincingly. I shall remember all the good points about my product. I tap the hidden reserves of mind power and shall close this sale successfully."

The first week he sold every customer he approached! He is now the district sales manager for his firm.

To tap your higher subconscious mind power, give yourself this meditation, as you hold your mind absolutely still:

I am now aware of my subconscious mind power. I relegate all automatic functions to its control. I withdraw my conscious mind from interfering with this higher power. I ask it to guide me to my right work. I wish to become a creative genius, to paint pictures, invent, write great stories, compose music. (Here you must substitute whatever creative gifts you desire. Do not limit yourself, for you can become proficient in many fields. Churchill was a statesman, but also a great writer, orator, painter and he had many other gifts.)

How a Woman Used This Meditation and Became a Sculptor

A thirty-five year old woman I once met in my lectures told me she was just an ordinary housewife, with no talent of any kind. I asked her what she would like to be, and she replied, "I would love to have been an artist, but I can't even draw a straight line!" I then told her of this Meditation for releasing creative genius and she began to use it daily. Within two weeks time she was impelled to enroll in a course in sculptoring that was being given by her church, and she soon found she had tremendous talent for art.

Meditation to Release Superconscious Mind Power

The third phase of superior mind power you can tap and release through your consciousness is that of the Superconscious mind. This was called by William James, of Harvard University, the Universal Mind. In mysticism it is referred to as the Cosmic Mind, which creates all things.

Sit quietly in meditation and meditate as follows:

I am aware of the supreme power back of the universe, which man calls God. I know that this Superior Mind created all things and sustains me. I now enter into the state of absorption with the light of God's Infinite Presence. My mind reflects His Mind, and I am aware of superior powers working through all levels of my consciousness. I am one with the light of Truth and truth reflects in my life. I am one with the light of Peace and my life is peaceful. I am one with the light of Joy and I reflect happiness in my daily life.

The Second Sacred Meditation

For a high degree of superior mental and spiritual power, the initiate in sacred meditation in the Yoga schools of philosophy, is taken into the second stage of absorption with the Light.

Sit in the stillness as before, and repeat the sacred Mantra *Ohm mane padme ohm.* When your mind is perfectly still indulge in contemplation of the mind on body and all its attributes.

Quietly project your thoughts into a rhythm, which is measured on the electro-encephalograph as between eight to twelve cycles per second and known as the Alpha state.

This is the meditation to use when you wish to achieve healing powers to overcome specific physical ailments. It is to be used to enhance the five senses so you will see, hear, feel, taste and smell with increased sensitivity.

This is the meditation to use when you wish to overcome some negative habit, such as smoking, alcoholism, or gambling.

As you sit in meditation, put yourself into the Alpha state by seeing the spiritual lake, without a ripple on its surface. Then with your eyes closed, say the following meditation. You may read this at first, until you memorize it, then, whenever you wish to achieve the Alpha state of meditation you may say this meditation:

I am now going into the Alpha state of meditation. I see the spiritual lake, and my mind becomes as peaceful and still as that lake.

I now contemplate the power of mind on body and all my five senses. I am aware of my mind in all its aspects. A higher power now flows through the creative centers of mind making me superior consciously and subconsciously. All the organs of my body now respond to this flow of cosmic mind power.

I contemplate my eyes and know that they are the perfect channels for my perception of the world about me. I now relax my conscious mind and let the higher power flow through my eyes, seeing everything perfectly.

When you meditate on the eyes, breathe deeply ten or fifteen times, sending the pranic life force up the spinal column and shoot-

ing it over the top of the head to the forefront of your head. At the
same time open the eyes and close them with the feeling that you are
shooting sparks through your eyeballs. This gently massages the
eyeball and helps contract and expand the optic lens, and helps improve the optic nerve which transmits the electrical impulses to the
higher brain, where true vision occurs.

This exercise in meditation has helped improve the vision of many
people I know. In dozens of cases of those who wore glasses for reading, it has improved their vision so much that they were able to read
perfectly without glasses!

Now do the same meditation for the sense of hearing. Contemplate
the ears and their function and say the following meditation:

> *I am aware of the sense of hearing. I now listen to every sound
> in my environment. I hear voices on the street, music at a dist-
> ance, the sounds of birds, crickets, and all of nature. My sense
> perceptions now become acute and my auditory nerve responds
> to the slightest vibrations in the atmosphere about me.*

How a Concert Violinist
Achieved High Sensitivity

A famous concert violinist whom I met in Carnegie Hall, when I
lectured there for years, has achieved a high degree of sensitivity
through this meditation. He produces sounds of such incredible beauty
that critics all praise him highly.

Each day choose a different sense perception for your meditation,
rotating them until you have achieved perfection in all five senses.

A dress designer achieved
great skill through meditation

I knew a dress designer who worked for one of the biggest studios
in Hollywood, who began Yoga Meditations in my classes, and gained
such proficiency in his trade that he could design gowns that were so
startling and different, he became one of Hollywood's highest paid
fashion designers.

The Third Absorption in the Light

Now you are ready to go into the third absorption in the light,
which you can achieve through daily meditation.

This meditation consists in contemplation on the cosmic virtues and qualities of mind.

Meditate on the first virtue for five minutes — TRUTH. Say the following meditation: "I now contemplate Truth. I reflect truth in my daily life. I am true to myself and to others. I recognize cosmic truth as the unifying principle back of the universe."

Good: For five minutes meditate on the quality of goodness as follows: "I now reflect good in my thoughts, words and deeds. God is good, and when I operate under the law of Goodness, I am Godly. My life prospers with good and I am aware that only good can overcome the negative power of evil."

Charity: Meditate on this virtue as follows for a few moments each day: "It is more blessed to give than to receive. I am now in the cosmic flow of good and my life is filled to overflowing with all the good things of life."

Beauty: Meditate a few moments each day on this quality, as follows: "I am aware of infinite beauty in all of nature. I am surrounded by God's golden presence in blooming flowers, green trees, blue skies, and distant mountains. I adorn my thoughts with beauty and I become beautiful. I register only that which is beautiful in my environment and ignore that which is ugly and debasing."

Compassion: I now meditate on this virtue, and my heart is compassionate for all living creatures. I am one with the vast brotherhood of all human beings. I give of my sympathy, consideration and kindness to others and I am in turn blessed with happiness, peace and abundance.

Love: Meditate on this virtue as follows: "I am aware of the divine emotion of love, in all its cosmic facets. God is love. I am one with infinite love. I love my fellowmen, and I reflect love daily in my relations with others."

A girl who could not find true love used this meditation

A twenty-three year old young lady once came to me complaining that she could not find true love. Every boy she went out with responded with a physical type of love that left her disgusted. I gave her this emotion of love to meditate on every day, and told her to say the words over and over, many times a day. She soon radiated a form of inner spiritual beauty that worked like a magnet to attract to her the higher type of man who was not interested in physical love alone. She became engaged to marry a fine young man within three months time!

How a Man Increased His Flow of Money Through Meditation

A man who told me he could never get enough money to get out of debt used two of these meditations, Good and Charity. He began to make himself a channel for good. He started the flow of riches and abundance by giving to others, and soon he had attracted twenty-five hundred dollars from an unexpected source. We magnetize that which we meditate on. Someone has said, "Show me a man's secret thoughts and I shall be able to predict the future events of his life."

The Fourth Absorption In the Light

The fourth and last absorption in the light is known as the meditation on Divine Ecstasy, in which one blends with the light. This is known as achieving the state of Nirvana, which is beyond pleasure or pain, and causes you to rise to the cosmic heights of meditation.

In this sacred meditation, light a white candle and prepare a shrine with some sacred relic that you believe in, such as a medal, a rosary, a cross or some other emblem of your faith in God.

You can have incense burning or some fragrant perfume. This helps in stimulating the higher centers of consciousness. In this meditation open the Three petals of the Sacred Lotus Blossom. Visualize the perfect multi-colored Lotus in all its perfection. This, in the Far East is a symbol of The Godhead in man, the ultimate perfection that resides within the immortal soul.

The First Petal that is opened in this meditation is one symbolical of the Omniscience of God. Meditate as follows:

> *I now open the sacred petal of omniscience. I am in the light of God's all-knowing, all-wise sacred presence.*
> *The secrets of the universe are now known to my higher mind. My soul is bathed by the golden light of cosmic spirit, and I enter into the divine romance where my soul shall dwell in perpetual union with the Light of God's infinite peace, infinite beauty, infinite good, infinite joy and infinite love.*

The second petal of the sacred lotus that you now open in meditation is that of Omnipresence. Again visualize the Lotus in all its multicolored loveliness. See the petals opening one by one, revealing the translucent beauty within that represents the imprisoned splendor of your soul. Meditate as follows, as you hold this picture in your mind of the perfection and beauty of the Lotus:

> *I now take on the omnipresence of infinite spirit that is every-where present and knows all things. I enter into that vast cosmic realm of infinite intelligence where my soul is transported to infinite bliss in a blending with the light of Nirvana. I am above all pleasure and pain. My body and its appetites is now under control. I am all mind and intellect and spirit. I am aware of the transcendental realm of pure spirit in which my soul is trans-ported to the celestial heights of love and ecstasy. I am one with the light.*

The third petal of the sacred lotus that you can now open in medita-tion is Omnipotence. Meditate as follows: God's infinite presence is everywhere present, in all things, and flowing through all creation in His glorious, golden Self.

I see His sublimity and His majesty in every towering mountain, in ever flowering bush and in every fragrant tree. I hear His voice in the falling rain, the thundering waterfall, the happy song of birds at eventide. I see His golden countenance in every incandescent sunrise and sunset, in the multi-colored, fragrant flowers that bedeck the face of earth, in the glittering moonlight and star-glow that illumines the purple mantle of night. In the cascading golden light of the sun which bathes the earth and causes all things to grow to nourish and sustain mankind, I am aware of His Power and His Might.

I recognize His Omnipotence, His Infinite Power, and my soul reflects this cosmic splendor and pays homage to His eternity. My soul now wears its mantle of immortality with sublimity and majesty and I am one with the Light of His Infinite Presence."

A Review of the Points in Chapter Nine

1. How the Masters or Gurus of the Far East achieve complete mastery of themselves and of life through Sacred Meditation.
2. The Cosmic Memory Bank which you may tap with your higher psychic mind centers and use hidden knowledge to shape the world of your choice.
3. How man grew wings of the soul and had revealed to him some of the greatest secrets in the universe.

4. The first sacred meditation: how to go into the first Absorption with the Light and achieve the meditation to open the higher mind centers that know all things.

5. How to use the Meditation known by science as the Theta brain wave pattern of from four to seven cycles per second, giving tremendous powers of the mind, like a genius.

6. How a college student used this meditation to improve his memory and passed at the head of his class.

7. A man used this Theta state of meditation and soon became a supersalesman, in which he sold every customer he approached in the first week of meditation and soon became sales manager for his firm.

8. How to use the powers of the conscious, subconscious and superconscious minds through the forces of meditation.

9. A housewife used this meditation to become a very talented artist and sculptor, without previous experience.

10. How to achieve the second sacred meditation known by science as the Alpha state of between twelve to eighteen brainwave cycles per second, to perform miracles of healing, to overcome bad habits and improve the mind.

11. How to contemplate on the power of mind and body and control all five senses, achieving better vision, more acute hearing, and improvement of all sense perceptions.

12. A concert violinist achieved a high degree of sensitivity and was acclaimed by the critics, when he had mastered this meditation on beauty.

13. How to achieve the third absorption in the light, through contemplation on the five virtues of Truth, Good, Charity, Beauty and Compassion and Love.

14. A girl was able to win perfect love after doing these meditations only a short time, and became engaged.

15. The fourth absorption in the light, and how to open the three sacred petals of the Lotus Blossom, Omniscience, Omnipresence and Omnipotence, to know all secrets of the universe and become one with the Golden light known as Nirvana, and finding release from pain and pleasure.

HOW TO OPEN THE SEVEN SACRED CHAKRAS OF CONSCIOUSNESS FOR ESP POWERS AND COSMIC PERCEPTION — 10

Transcendental meditation can be used to give you amazing powers of the mind and soul. There are seven sacred chakras of consciousness which have their location in the brain and body. When these are opened through the proper meditations, you will have instant powers of extra sensory perception, you will possess cosmic perception, and astral vision that gives you the ability to know secrets denied to ordinary mortals.

In this chapter we shall investigate this most profound mystery from the mysticism of the Far East, and learn how to enhance psychic powers that make you supernormal.

Before learning how to open these seven sacred chakras through meditation, it is important that you understand man is a three-fold being.

The physical body, with its material needs, often makes demands on the mind for its care and guidance. When the physical self is allowed to rule the consciousness, man is no better off than animals, who follow the dictates of their physical appetites only.

When man learns how to control this physical body with its incessant demands, and rises into a higher strata of consciousness, he is freed of the body's aches and pains and constant complaints. This is what Yogas attempt to do through the opening of the seven sacred chakras — to relegate to each area of the mind and body, its proper control, so the soul of man is free and can follow its divine promptings and achieve spiritual illumination.

How a Woman Bound With Earthly
Troubles Suffered Needlessly

A woman I once knew suffered constantly from all kinds of complaints. Not only was she suffering physically, but she was undergoing mental torture as well. She took many different types of medicines for her physical ailments. She went to a psychiatrist at a cost of twenty-five dollars a visit, for her mental anguish, and she beseiged her church minister for his aid in helping her solve her spiritual problems of mental guilt and soul anguish.

There is no need of going into the nature of her many complaints, but she was a slave to her body and its incessant needs. I gave her this method for opening the seven sacred chakras of mind, body and soul, and the proper meditations for each. She began to use them daily for only fifteen minutes, and soon she was mentally, physically and spiritually unified and healed perfectly.

This branch of Yoga control is known as the Rajah or Royal Yoga, and deals with opening the higher centers of consciousness through a rigid system of mind control, breathing and meditation.

THE REGIMEN TO USE FOR OPENING THE
SEVEN SACRED CHAKRAS
THROUGH MEDITATION

1. The first chakra is located in the vital zone below the navel, controlling the organs of reproduction and the vital life force.

The physical function of this chakra is for purposes of perpetuating the human race through reproduction. However, the emotions generated through this vital zone are often misused and degenerate into animalism, passion and lust, making man a slave to his basic sex nature.

How a Young Man Ruined His Life
Through Ignorance of Chakras Laws

Ignorance of the spiritual laws and the true purpose of the sexual instinct in man, can often bring ruination to a person's life.

A young man of twenty-two came to me in real trouble. Two girls he had dated, were both pregnant, and he didn't know what to do.

His uncontrolled passions in each instance had led him to lie to them, telling them he was going to marry them. "Now," he told me, "neither girl knows about the other. I can't marry them both, and I'm not sure that I love either of them. What in the world can I do?"

I told him it would be wrong for him to escape his responsibilities and yet, he could not marry either girl. I advised him to confess the truth to the girls, and admit that he had lied to them about marriage, telling them about the other girl.

He followed my advice and confessed his deception to each of the girls. They both turned on him and refused to have anything further to do with him, but this did not solve the problem of their pregnancy. After seeking counsel from their family physicians, each girl decided on her own, to have an abortion. The young man agreed to pay for this expense but the moral guilt that he incurred will haunt him throughout his entire life and cloud any future marriage with fear of detection and other possible repercussions. He solved his problem but he is spiritually guilty of violating basic cosmic laws and he must pay a Karmic debt throughout his lifetime.

How to Open the First Chakra

As you sit in quiet meditation, with your eyes closed, concentrate your attention to the vital zone. See the sacred lotus blossom, and mentally open three petals, meditating on the color Red, and ascribe to the three petals the qualities of Love, Inspiration and Ecstasy.

Say or think the following meditation:

I am now aware of the cosmic fire within my mind and body. It is now directed into its proper sphere of action as creative life force and energy. I sublimate this celestial fire into the divine emotion of love, ennobling, elevating and refining all my senses, and causing me to rise above lust, animalism and sensuality.

I sublimate this divine emotion into inspiration and ecstasy. I become a creative channel and express great ideas for the good of the world. I express love unselfishly to all people and I am inspired to great creative deeds through this noble passion of love.

A widow used this meditation to become a social worker

A fifty-five year old widow was lost in grief when I first met her. She wore black perpetually in mourning for her husband. She did not know what to do or where to go. A friend brought her to one of my lectures where I told about how one can sublimate love into the spiritual realm of action. She told me later that she did not want to marry again, but she wanted to have some kind of creative activity. I gave her this meditation to use and after two weeks she returned and told me the answer had come through in meditation. She was guided to do social work with underprivileged children. She had never had a family of her own and she was starved for love. Sublimating the emotion of love into this work gave this woman great happiness, and perhaps one day, she will stop grieving for her husband and find some man she can love and marry.

2. The second chakra is located in the naval region, the stomach area. This section rules the physical and material body, with its appetite for food, its conversion of food into mental energy and creative ideas.

When this chakra holds man earthbound, a slave to his desire for food, he becomes a glutton, and suffers from all kinds of negative effects.

The purpose of this meditation is to elevate this chakra into its mental and spiritual equivalent, elevating man above the realm of animalism and physical appetites.

To open this second chakra, sit in quiet meditation, and direct your thoughts into the region of the stomach. Be aware of the true purpose and function of this vital area. It is to sustain man physically and give him power to remain healthy and strong, so he can fulfill his life function.

Visualize the sacred lotus blossom, and ascribe five petals to this chakra, with the color orange. The five petals that you will open in this chakra are: Life, Vitality, Growth, Youth, Creativity.

Meditate as follows for opening this second Chakra:

I now open the second chakra of consciousness. I am in attunement with the life force. My appetites are now under control of my higher mind. I transmute physical force and energy into a stream of youth and vitality that causes me to fulfill my life goal perfectly. I grow and evolve mentally, physically and spiritually. I now convert this physical force into creativity to shape my life destiny. I release my physical energy into creative ideas of beauty, constructive good and cosmic perfection.

3. The third sacred chakra is located in the solar plexus, or what is known as the diaphragm. This is located a little above the stomach area, and controls the vital function of breathing and life prana.

To open this chakra ascribe four petals of the lotus blossom to it, and the color green. The four petals that you will now meditate on opening are: Energy, Faith, Joy and Hope. As this area controls the life prana or breath, when you meditate draw in the breath to the count of four and hold it, count four, and then release it as a deep sigh. Then meditate as follows:

I now inhale the pranic life force through my breath. Breath is life and I now express energy that flows to all my brain and body cells and makes me aware of power. I have faith in the creative principle that gave me life, and I express that faith daily in my life. I am joyous with the flame of life, and I become infused with the creative spirit of joy. I now express hope for the future and am optimistic and radiant, in the knowledge that I am in tune with the creative spirit of the universe.

How a Woman Rejected by Husband Renewed Her Life

A woman who had lost her purpose for living, when she lost the love of her husband to another woman, came to me extremely depressed. She announced that life had ended for her. She was emotionally distraught and had even considered suicide.

I put her on this meditation for opening the third chakra, and within a week she came into my office, filled with boundless energy and hope for her future. She did the meditation three times daily, with the breathing. She meditated on the four petals of the lotus, Energy, Faith, Joy and Hope, and for the first time in weeks felt wonderful. She accepted an invitation from a male acquaintance to go to a party and she danced until midnight. She told me when I next saw her, "That meditation kindled a new spark in my heart and soul. I can see my way clear to falling in love again with a man and once more being joyous!"

4. The fourth sacred chakra is located in the heart area and is known as the heart wheel. To it ascribe the color of crimson red, and open six petals of the Lotus: Love, Loyalty, Sincerity, Optimism, Charity, Forgiveness.

To open this sacred chakra sit in meditation and say or think the following:

> *I now direct the pranic life force to the heart wheel. This is the center of my life energy and force. I live and breathe and radiate the life force to everyone I meet. I express the divine emotion of love. I open the petals of the sacred lotus and reveal the jewel in the heart of the lotus. I take on the quality of loyalty and sincerity. I am charitable and forgiving in my attitude towards others. I become optimistic and cheerful as I survey my future, knowing that the divine emotion of love controls and regulates all my life functions. I am peaceful and serene in the midst of life's problems.*

How a Man with Heart Trouble
Used This Meditation for Recovering Health

A fifty-eight year old man came to my attention who had already had two heart attacks. He had dangerously high blood pressure. He was highly nervous and irritable and could hardly sit at his desk all day. He lost his temper quickly and flew into fits of rage. When I met him he was red-faced, his breath came in short gasps and his eyes had a wild, frightened look.

I knew that this man was suffering from the modern sickness that has afflicted millions of our citizens in the United States. Fear, anxiety and mental pressure were taking their toll yearly in hundreds of thousands dying unnecessarily from heart trouble and related ailments.

He took my lectures and lessons for two months, and learned about the miracles that medical men in the laboratories were performing with the new Alpha brain wave therapy, in which they put their patients into deep states of meditation.

This man worked on the fourth chakra especially, controlling the heart wheel. He said the meditation faithfully several times a day, and began to visualize his heart beating normally, as he opened and closed his fist to the count of seventy-two beats a minute, simulating the heart action. He was soon able to bring his heart action down to normal and his blood pressure decreased to nearly normal.

Within three months time you would not know this was the same man who had come to me in desperation, on the verge of death! He became calm and peaceful. His complexion was no longer a beefy red, but became a normal, healthy color. But the greatest results were to be observed by his doctor when he gave him an electrocardiogram — the doctor could hardly believe the miracle he was witnessing — the man's heart action was normal and there was not the slightest evidence he had ever had a heart attack! Truly, he had performed a miracle!

5. The fifth sacred chakra is located in the base of the throat area. To this meditation ascribe the color of sunlight yellow, and open the following five petals of the Lotus Bloom: Power, Dignity, Pride, Honesty, and dynamic action.

As the throat is the connecting medium between the brain and body, it is a vitally important area. Here it is that the entrance to the lungs as well as to all the vital organs exists. This chakra has repercussions throughout the entire body. Speech is formed in this area, through the vocal chords. Man's noblest expression of lofty thoughts occurs through words, which are formed from the passageway leading from the lungs to the lips.

Meditate as follows, as you visualize the opening of the five petals of the lotus:

> *I now open the fifth sacred chakra, which is the gateway to mental and physical power. I project this power now to my brain, releasing its golden light to the creative centers of my consciousness. I am aware of the magical power of words with their command of life's forces. I now express pride and dignity in my evolved state of consciousness, which differentiates me from lowly animals. I rise to the heights of spiritual awareness and practice the virtue of honesty and truth, as I release the pranic life force to this area. Dynamic action, mental and physical, now is released, causing my life to be directed into channels of productivity and beauty.*

A famous opera star uses this meditation

A very famous opera star I once met in concert at Carnegie Hall some years ago, told me she was having some difficulty in producing her high notes. She was about forty years of age, and feared that time was taking its toll of her magnificent voice. I discovered that her tenseness, from fear, was causing her vocal chords to be strained. I gave her this meditation on the fifth chakra to use to release her throat from tension. She practiced the meditation for fifteen minutes before going on stage. It achieved miraculous results and she went on singing much longer than she might have if she had not practiced this chakra.

I have given this meditation to actors, ministers and priests, salesmen, who need to talk all day. I have seen teachers that must talk each day for several hours, suddenly release tension through this meditation and never tire in their work. It is a most valuable meditation and has many other repercussions that profoundly affect the higher creative centers of consciousness.

6. The sixth sacred chakra is located in the area between the eyes. Ascribe to this Chakra the astral color of mauve or orchid, and the following five petals of the Lotus: Beauty, Friendliness, Generosity, Happiness and Radiance.

This area is known in mystic philosophy, as the third eye, where psychic vision can be aroused. In meditation try to visualize this third eye in the forefront of the brain, and meditate as follows:

> *I now open the third eye of psychic and astral vision and project the pranic life force to my eyes and head region. I now see with the inner eye, and am aware of the true spiritual reality of all life. I meditate on beauty and my life becomes beautiful. I open the petal of friendliness and I attract friends and loved ones who share with me their good. I become generous and do good for others, and receive blessings from everyone I meet. I glow with happiness and radiance and I magnetize the centers of my consciousness so I attract only happy and wonderful experiences.*

How an Introvert Became Socially
Popular Through Meditation

A girl of nineteen was extremely shy and withdrawn. She had gone through a painful adolescence, in which she fell in love with a boy who ignored her. She was afraid to date boys, for she felt awkward and self-conscious dancing, and imagined that everyone was looking at her and laughing at her because she was so gawky.

Her mother brought her to a series of classes I was doing in New York on Meditation. She learned about the opening of the seven chakras, especially this sixth one, and she began to practice the meditation, projecting the five qualities of the Lotus, Beauty, Friendliness, Generosity, Happiness and Radiance, and within two weeks this girl changed her entire attitude towards life. As she changed, people reacted differently towards her and soon she was dating boys regularly and enjoying a new and wonderful social life.

7. The seventh sacred chakra is located in the crown of the head and is known as the Crown Chakra. The color for this chakra is gold, and the five petals of the lotus to be opened in meditation are: Aspiration, Inspiration, Idealization, Cosmic Awareness, and Soul's Elevation.

> *I now project my concentration to the crown chakra, where reside all the powers of my mind and spirit. I breathe deeply and project the golden pranic life force up my spinal column to the base of my head, where it gushes like a golden fountain of light, illuminating my mind, my imagination, my memory, my psychic centers, are all now opening and releasing their spiritual forces for my guidance.*
>
> *I now meditate on aspiration, and mentally climb the spiritual mountain top where my consciousness is expanded to embrace the entire cosmos. I breathe deeply and as I inspire the life prana, I am lifted on wings of inspiration to the loftiest ideas that man may achieve. I idealize all my life experience, striving to uplift, ennoble, dignify and beautify every thought and experience in my life. I achieve a state of cosmic awareness and I am one with infinite intelligence, infinite beauty, infinite good, infinite joy, and infinite love.*
>
> *Now my soul has reached its zenith in mystical elevation and I am one with the cosmic mind. I am in harmony with all of life's highest spiritual forces and I have entered through the Golden Door of Brahma into a blending with the Light. The Light is All.*

Review of Chapter Ten

1. How the opening of the seven sacred chakras through meditation can give you amazing powers of the mind and soul.

2. How an earth-bound woman suffered pain and agony, and learned how to elevate herself above her problems through using meditation on the seven chakras.

3. How to open the first chakra and use it to overcome animalism, lust and misapplied sexual energy.

4. A young man of twenty-two misused this sexual power and became involved with two young women, who brought him misery and guilt.

5. A widow of fifty-five was miserable at loss of her husband, until she learned how to open the first chakra, and then she was guided to go into social work, where she found happiness.

6. The second chakra that rules the appetites and the hunger urge, and how to elevate this into a creative sphere of action that keeps one from becoming gluttonous and animalistic.

7. How to open the third chakra, which controls the vital function of breathing and life prana and elevate this area to creative action, energy, faith, joy and hope.

8. How a woman used this chakra to build a new life and fall in love again, when she had been hopelessly lonely.

9. The fourth sacred chakra, the heart wheel, where all emotions are centered, and how to control the heart, the blood pressure, and the vital functions of the body to achieve peace, health and happiness.

10. A fifty-eight year old man with a severe heart ailment used this meditation to overcome his condition. His doctors pronounced that his healing was truly a miracle.

11. How to open the fifth chakra, in the throat region, and release power, dignity, pride, honesty and dynamic action.

12. A famous opera singer used this meditation at forty years of age and overcame strain in her vocal chords and continued her career for many years after.

13. How to open the sixth chakra located between the eyes, and release the qualities of beauty, friendliness, generosity, happiness and radiance in your personality.

14. A girl of nineteen was an introvert and miserable until she learned how to open this chakra and release these

qualities. She was soon dating boys and changed her personality.

15. The seventh sacred chakra in the crown of the head and how to open the five petals of the lotus that bring you Aspiration, Inspiration, Idealization, Cosmic Awareness and the Soul's Elevation into the state of Nirvana or blending with the Light.

HOW TO BUILD THE GOLDEN AURA OF MAGNETIC ATTRACTION TO ACHIEVE A GREAT DESTINY

11

There is a magnetic power in the invisible universe, which you may tap through transcendental meditation, and surround yourself with a golden aura that literally makes you a magnet. When this golden aura is charged with dynamic mystic power, you can magnetize and attract to yourself fame, friends, fortune, and thrilling life experiences.

Have you ever observed some people on whom fate seems to smile? They are charming and attractive to everyone. They have a host of friends. They are invited everywhere, and they always seem to do everything with great ease. Such people seem to become famous without effort. They become rich, because they are darlings of good luck and everyone wants to do something for them. We look at such people and say, "They were born under a lucky star!"

For many years. when I was known as the adviser to the Hollywood Stars, I used this magnetic principle, which I called the Magic Circle, to make stars of truck drivers, elevator operators and sales clerks. I witnessed the miracle of transformation which took place when I put these unknown players into states of meditation, and helped them build the golden aura of magnetic attraction.

Some of the great stars who have this magic circle aura, and who have kept their fame and youthful appearance throughout the years are: Bette Davis, Gloria Swanson, Joan Crawford, Susan Hayward, Jimmy Durante, Bob Hope, Lucille Ball, Elizabeth Taylor, and many many others to whom I gave the golden aura of magnetic attraction when they were young. Photographs which I have with these and hundreds of others, shows them to be in their early twenties when I gave them this priceless mystic secret, and they have never lost throughout the years their charm, magnetism, and money making ability.

SCIENTIFIC PROOF OF A MYSTERIOUS MAGNETIC PROPERTY

Now there is scientific proof that there is in the universe a mysterious magnetic property that ties all things together in the universe.

This magnetic field of attraction is what holds our earth up in space, causing it to rotate around the sun. The moon, is attracted into the magnetic orbit of the earth and circles in its magic aura, held by the earth's magnetism.

You possess this same invisible, mysterious magnetism within your brain and body. When you have this magnetic power strongly, you attract into your orbit of life experiences all the good, rich and fortunate experiences that you hold in your consciousness. You can build this magic circle of magnetism and make it stronger, through a regime of meditation, breathing and positive thoughts. In this chapter we shall explore this method fully and learn how to use it to magnetize your aura and make you charming, magnetic, and attractive.

THE BRAIN WAVE CYCLE KNOWN AS BETA

In the scientific laboratory, through using the brain wave machine, it has now been found that the state of meditation which produces this magnetic aura in the human body and brain is known as Beta. This is when the brain waves have been accelerated to fourteen to twenty-eight cycles per second. This Beta state is faster than Alpha, which is from eight to twelve cycles per second, and is also faster than the Theta state which is from four to seven cycles per second. However, it is slower than the Delta, which is from twenty-eight to thirty-five cycles per second.

To put your brain waves into this rhythm, and build your magnetic field of attraction, you must go into meditation daily and actually create the golden aura around your body. This process of daily exercise magnetizes your mind and your body, making you a magnet which attracts into your aura anything you put into your consciousness.

HOW TO BUILD THE GOLDEN AURA OF MAGNETIC ATTRACTION TO ACHIEVE A GREAT DESTINY

1. When you go into meditation to create the Beta state, it is necessary that you meditate on those things that will actually stimulate your brain centers and accelerate the rhythm of the brain. Stored within the convolutions of your brain are vast funds of magnetism, lying dormant, awaiting your command to spring into motion.

When you have creative action in your mind centers and arouse yourself to tremendous activity mentally, you are creating magnetism.

THE FIVE MEDITATIONS OF MAGNETIC AROUSAL

A. Desire: When you arouse your mind through the emotion of desire, tremendous magnetism is released which floods your brain centers and flows to your body, expressing itself as creative action. You will be driven by magnetic and electrical impulses from your brain to your nerves and muscles, in the direction of that which you desire.

Desire success, and magnetize it by going into meditation for five minutes as follows: "I now magnetize the element of success and arouse my brain centers with the thought that I shall become a great success. I wish to become famous, well-known, popular, and sought after by others. I now project magnetism to my personality and become like a magnet, attracting success on every plane."

A young man magnetized his brain centers with the creative idea and desire that he would become a famous baseball player. He had worked for me as an usher at my lectures in California, and he believed that he could achieve whatever he could conceive, as he often heard me say at lectures and classes. He began to say his meditations daily until desire was raised to such a fever pitch that he attracted a man who was very big in one of the baseball clubs on the Coast. Through this contact this young man was given training, as he was naturally athletically inclined, and within six months he was given a position as first baseman on one of the minor leagues. Within another year there was an opening on one of the major leagues and this young man became one of its most successful players!

B. High Purpose or Motivation: Magnetism is created in your brain centers when you have a high purpose for living. This is called motivation, and when you are impelled towards some goal for some specific reason you generate more magnetism or attraction power in your aura. There are two forces in gravity, which is magnetic attraction, between the earth and other planets: One is the force known as attraction, the other is repulsion. When you put more positive magnetism into your aura, and less of the negative, you become more attractive and magnetic.

If you have a desire for only money, you may attract money, but you are apt to lose out on other values in life.

Have a desire to help others; to share your good. Want to make a fortune so you can give your family benefits. When you want success and money to elevate the standards of the world, you will be given more magnetic attraction to achieve your high goal. The great geniuses of history had this type of unselfish motivation to spur them on to great achievement.

A Woman Educated Three Children through This Power

A woman whose husband died in an accident, had three children and no money with which to support them. She had studied some of my lectures on meditation and learned about having a master motive in her life. She knew that the future of her three children was all important to her, and she set this as her motivation for future action. Each day she went into the Beta state of meditation, and gave herself the following statement:

> *I now ask for higher guidance to my future destiny. I want to help my children achieve an education, so they will attain their life goals. I want to be useful to the world and help elevate its standards to greater perfection.*

On the second week of her meditations she felt that something was going to happen soon that would solve her problem. She had occasion to go to a lawyer to handle the matter of her husband's will. He had left an insurance policy of a few thousand dollars, and some personal effects, leaving his wife as the Executrix. When she obtained the five thousand dollars from the policy, the lawyer asked her how she was going to invest it. She replied that she did not know, as she had no experience in investments. The lawyer told her he had been approached by two men with ten thousand dollars who needed another five thousand dollars, to open an offset printing shop, and he suggested she go into the venture. This woman was made an equal partner in the firm, and she was able to spend her days there while her children were at school. The offset printing became such a tremendous success that in a few months time she had her original investment back and received from that time on, one-third of the profits!

How to Meditate On A High Master Motive

When you go into meditation have some specific thing you wish to accomplish, such as making money to pay some debts, or the mortgage on your home; to educate your children, to buy a business, so you will have financial security. Then as you sit in the stillness, accelerate your brain waves to the Beta state of from fourteen to twenty-eight cycles per second. This is done by exciting the brain centers with some new and exciting information, or pressing the imagination into service and visualizing the things you want to accomplish.

Think or say to yourself the following meditation:

> *I now magnetize the centers of my consciousness with thoughts of great success. I contemplate the future with joy and expectation of my good. I wish to attract money to achieve my life goal. I wish to help my family achieve a better way of life. I visualize myself in my own business. I see myself making money and spending it to improve my family's life. I now project the creative magnetism to achieve the great destiny that I desire.*

C. Enthusiasm: The emotion of enthusiasm is extremely good for magnetic arousal of the higher mind centers. Each day before beginning your day's activity, magnetize your mind with this powerful emotion. A child's enthusiasm for life is what gives it such creative energy. Your blood sugar energy increases when you go into this state of meditation that arouses enthusiasm for life. Energy flows to your brain and body cells and magnetism is released when you meditate as follows:

> *I now release into my aura the magnetic quality of enthusiasm. I thrill with the joy of life. I am aware of the mystical purpose back of my existence. I now ask for higher guidance to my true*

*destiny. I am joyous and expectant of my good. I share my
enthusiasm with everyone I meet.*

Say this over five or ten times before each day's activity begins,
and carry this aura of magnetic enthusiasm with you throughout the
day.

A young man used this meditation for one week daily, when he
went out to apply for a position as a junior executive with a large
manufacturing firm. He faced competition from ten other young men,
with college diplomas, and as presentable and capable as he was. He
was chosen above the others. Later he asked the personnel director
why he had selected him, and the man replied, "You were so cheerful and optimistic. I admired your youthful enthusiasm for the job
and I knew if you brought that quality into your work you would be
the best man for our firm."

D. Imagination: To build a magnetic aura and attract into your
experience great and unusual events, you must utilize the gift of
imagination.

Each day meditate on releasing this quality. Go into your meditation period and hold in your mind two different states of consciousness. Visualize something ugly and unpleasant. This is a negative
picture and short-circuits your mental and physical magnetism. Then
visualize something beautiful and inspiring. This builds a positive
magnetic charge in the storage batteries of your mind.

Then carry this meditation into action by saying or thinking:

*I now use the law of spiritual transmutation to change that
which is ugly into that which is beautiful. I am filled with the
concept of beauty and I reflect the magnetism of creative
imagination in my personality, my voice, my facial expression
and in my atmosphere.*

Then for five minutes meditate on the most beautiful things you
can recall; a sunrise or sunset scene; the grandeur of a mountain
range capped with a mantle of snow; the most beautiful springtime
you can remember with multi-colored blooms and verdant trees in a
peaceful valley. Mentally stand beside the seashore and look to the
flaming western sky, with its gold and crimson reflecting in the tranquil sea and let this memory color your imagination with beauty.

As you build your inner concept of the greatest and most beautiful
experiences in your life, you will magnetize your mind centers with

these forces and you will then attract to yourself the life experiences you image.

How a Woman Visualized a Home In Florida

A woman in our lecture work in New York City, was resentful of the cold winters she had endured for years. She began to meditate on palm trees, perpetual golden sunshine and a Shangri-la of eternal beauty and peace. She kept up her meditation and visualization for three months, using only five minutes a day to project this idealistic concept of where she wished to live.

At the end of that time her husband was transferred by his firm to Fort Lauderdale, Florida, and she found herself living in the little stucco house, facing the sea, in a pageant of tropical flowers and vegetation, just as she had imagined it in her periods of daily meditation!

E. **Emotional Intensity:** You can build a magnetic and attractive aura if you meditate a few moments daily on emotional intensity. Just as when a violin is tuned correctly, it gives beautiful music, so too when the human psyche is attuned to the positive emotions of joy, peace, charity, forgiveness, good, truth, and love, the subtle wavelengths that are set into motion from the brain, reflect in the aura magnetism, charm and power.

Of all human emotions that give intensity to the aura, Love is, perhaps, the most magnetic and powerful. This is why one of the most magnetic mystics of all time said, "A new commandment I give unto you: that ye love one another." This magnetic command sets into motion magnetic vibrations in the human aura that wipe away all hatred, suspicion and enmity.

In daily meditation run through the magnet of your mind all the positive, magnetic emotions as follows:

> *I meditate on joy and radiate in my aura emotions of friendliness and good cheer towards all humanity.*
>
> *I magnetize my mind centers with the emotion of peace. I dwell in peace with the entire world and radiate serenity and joy to every person I meet.*
>
> *I concentrate my thoughts on being charitable and kind. I share my good with others and I am blessed with abundance.*
>
> *I magnetize my mind centers with sympathy, understanding and forgiveness of others. I am tolerant of the weaknesses of others and forgive them for their unkind words and acts.*

I am surrounded by the magnetic aura of good. I attract only good and beautiful experiences in my life.

I radiate the magnetism of truth. I am true to myself and shape my destiny by the highest ideals of truth, honesty and high morality.

I meditate on the different aspects of love and I become loving and beloved by all people. I love God and I now serve Him and humanity in loving service and with joy.

Sir Francis Chichester sailed around the world in the *Gypsy Moth,* and all the world marveled at the courage of this man, nearly seventy years of age, who could, single-handedly dare do alone, what most men half his age could never have accomplished. Later, when he was asked on national television his philosophy of life, Sir Francis said, "To live life with intensity, intensifies life." This man, who was later knighted by his Queen, hit on one of the great secrets of life and magnetism in that statement.

Your brain centers come to life with magnetic action that radiates in your personality, and causes you to do great things, when you put into the convolutions of your brain the emotional intensity of great and courageous thoughts, daring and inspired actions, high and noble ideals, and when you express these daily in your life, you achieve a truly great destiny.

Review of Pointers in Chapter Eleven

1. How to magnetize a golden aura of good luck, charm and attractiveness around yourself, that works like a magnet, bringing you fame, fortune, friends and riches.
2. Some of the great Hollywood stars that have used my system of the golden magic circle meditation and achieved outstanding success throughout the years.
3. How to create the brain wave cycle known by scientists as Beta, which causes you to create great quantities of magnetism and which gives you the golden aura of success and greatness.
4. The first meditation for arousing magnetism within your brain and releasing it in your Aura, is the Emotion of Desire.
5. How a young man magnetized his brain centers with creative ideas that made him into a famous baseball player.
6. How to use the great motivation of high purpose for achieving

a great destiny, and building the magnetic quality of attraction in your aura.

7. A woman, left a widow early in life, was able to meditate on achieving success through this method and built a fortune that helped educate her family, and give them security.

8. How to meditate on a high master motive and excite your brain centers into creative and inspiring action.

9. How to use the arousing emotion of enthusiasm to release magnetic energy in your aura and build a bright destiny.

10. How one young man was able to win a position over ten competitors because he had an aura of good cheer and optimism, through meditating on these qualities daily.

11. How the power of a vivid imagination helps shape your destiny and creates the conditions you image within your mind.

12. A woman used this meditation to create a tropical paradise for herself, when she could not stand the cold winters of New York city.

13. How to build the golden aura of magnetism through emotional intensity, and the positive emotions of joy, peace, charity, forgiveness, good, truth and love, which are the most magnetic emotions to use in daily meditation.

THE TEN POSITIVE STAGES OF MEDITATION THAT CAN PERFORM MIRACLES IN YOUR LIFE

12

Through transcendental meditation you can literally become a miracle worker. A miracle is something that is achieved through the release of supernormal powers. Your higher centers of consciousness radiate tremendous creative power when your conscious mind is removed from the scene of action. The Yogas achieved this suspension of the interfering conscious mind by withdrawing the sense perceptions, through a meditation, which was similar to self-hypnosis, and then through meditation, they were able to arouse whatever brain centers were needed to achieve the miracle they desired.

THE TEN AREAS OF CONSCIOUSNESS THAT GIVE YOU MIRACLE WORKING POWERS

There are ten areas of consciousness that you can arouse through meditation, that can give you miracle working powers. These are:

1. For memory retention and total recall.
2. For concentration, visualization and imagination.
3. For solving problems through rationalization.
4. For attracting success and financial security.
5. For releasing creative ideas and inspiration.

6. For physical healing, youth and vitality.
7. For elevating the consciousness to superior mental action.
8. For attracting your soul mate in love and marriage.
9. For intuition and psychic phenomena.
10. For cosmic fulfillment and spiritual completion.

USE THE FOLLOWING REGIMEN OF MEDITATION TO AROUSE THE MIRACLE WORKING POWERS OF CONSCIOUSNESS

1. For Memory Retention and Total Recall of the Past

Go into the state of meditation known as Theta, in which your brain will release its powers on a slow wave length of from four to seven cycles per second.

To slow your brain waves down to this rhythm, it is necessary that you fix your attention on one thing at a time. Memory retention is possible only when you make an effort to fix an image in your mind, by concentrating all the powers of your mind on the object or fact you want to remember.

When you go into the Theta state of meditation, close your eyes and visualize a tortoise, with its slow movements and deliberate actions. It is never in a hurry, but slowly ambles on its way. Now, in contrast to the tortoise, think of a rabbit, darting here and there rapidly. The rabbit can be likened to the Alpha state of meditation, where the brain waves are from twelve to eighteen cycles per second. Such a rapid wave length does not stop to fix things in consciousness, for it flits from one thought to another without pause.

Also, to create the Theta brain wave length, you can visualize an hour glass with grains of sand trickling through it one at a time. This meditation will slow down the stream of consciousness, making it possible to focus your attention on one thing at a time and retaining its mental image, before going on to another thought.

A business executive used this technique successfully

A business executive came to my lectures in New York City, complaining that he had a very poor memory. In his work it was necessary that he remember many important facts, which he found he could not do easily.

I showed him how to go into the Theta state of meditation and file all incoming data through his five senses, with this meditation:

> *I now concentrate all my faculties of mind on one thing at a time. I observe the world around me. I concentrate on sight. I see one thing at a time and I register what I see.*
>
> *I concentrate on hearing. I hear one thing at a time and I am aware of what I hear. I now store it in my memory bank for future reference and recall.*
>
> *I am now aware of my sense of touch, and feel one thing at a time, registering the sensation in my higher mind.*
>
> *I am aware of taste, and concentrate all my powers of mind on what I taste, remembering and recalling that which I wish to fix in consciousness.*
>
> *I am concentrating on the sense of smell, and will retain that which I wish to remember.*

As he carefully fixed in his memory centers each of his five senses, he became a more discriminating person in relation to what was going on in the world around him. When he needed to remember a fact, or a name, he would stop and fix it in his memory centers in the same way. Within one month's time this man became a repository of thousands of new facts, names and memory patterns which improved his efficiency and made his work more enjoyable.

2. For Concentration, Visualization and Imagination

This state of meditation is used for building the powers of your conscious and subconscious minds so you can more easily solve problems, select the events of your life, and release new creative patterns of imagination in your daily activities.

For this type of meditation go into the Alpha state of consciousness, which is from eight to twelve cycles per second.

Sit quietly in meditation. Relax your body and your mind completely, by letting go of all worries, anxieties, and fears. Say to yourself over and over: Peace, be still. Be still and know that I am God. Then mentally visualize the spiritual lake, peaceful and still, without a ripple on its surface.

Now you are ready to go into your meditation. Think or say the following words to yourself:

I am now in a state of absolute calm and peace. I fix my thoughts on my mind. I am aware of my imagination. I now create the new patterns of events that I wish in my life. I visualize myself being successful and prosperous. I image the type of person I wish to be. I concentrate all my faculties on cultivating new talents for creative work. I release mind power to my everyday affairs, solving all problems and achieving control of my mind, nerves, body and environment.

How a College Student Got to Remember

A girl in college had a problem in concentrating on what her teachers said. Also, when she read something, her mind skimmed over the words but she found herself not able to retain a thing she read. She came to me deeply troubled, but her problem was that she did not know how to focus her mind power on what she was doing.

I put her into the Theta state of meditation and she began to practice this daily for two weeks. She returned at the end of that time radiant with joy. She said, "It is amazing. Now I read and remember everything I read." Soon she was getting progressively better grades in her school work.

How an Advertising Man Got New Ideas

A commerical artist, who did advertising layouts for newspapers, worked in one of New York City's biggest department stores. He had such a scarcity of new ideas in his work that he began to worry about losing his job. I showed him how to go into the Theta state of meditation, and open new creative centers of consciousness. He reported tremendous progress the first week, and after one month, so many new ideas came through that he won promotion and an increase in salary!

3. For Solving Problems
Through Rationalization

To open centers of consciousness to solve problems, you must go into the meditation known as the Beta state, where your brain waves are accelerated from fourteen to twenty-eight cycles per second.

To go into the Beta state, breathe deeply, and increase your breathing, expelling the air dynamically between your lips with a sound like the put-put-put of a motor boat. After you have done this dynamic breathing about ten or fifteen times, you will feel a sense of fullness in your head, and your heart will begin to beat a little more rapidly than formerly. You will then be in the Beta state of meditation.

Hold this meditation in consciousness and say or think these words to yourself:

> *I now enter into the Beta state of meditation. Increase my mind's action and perception. I now call on my higher faculties of reasoning and rationalization to give me the solution to the following problem.*

Then bring the problem into the forefront of consciousness, dwelling on its several aspects briefly, without emotion, but coldly and calmly, as thought it were a problem in arithmetic that you are trying to solve.

How a Woman Sold Worthless
Desert Land for A Fortune

A woman in my Los Angeles lecture group told me how she used this meditation to help her solve a worrisome problem.

She had inherited a seemingly worthless tract of desert land near Los Angeles, from her mother. Everyone thought the old woman was crazy when she bought the land, but she confidently held it until the time of her death.

Her daughter held the land for many years, although many times she was tempted to stop paying taxes on it, for everyone told her it was worthless. There was no water on the land, and it was not good for grazing cattle or anything else.

When this woman learned about meditation, she asked her higher mind what she should do with this land, try to sell it, or hold it? She got the answer to hold it.

A few months later the government announced plans to build an irrigation system in that section of the desert, and she sold her land for a profit of $100,000!

4. For Attracting Success
and Financial Security

For this form of meditation, I have developed a state of consciousness which I call the Gamma state of meditation. This goes beyond the four known realms that have been tested in the scientific laboratories and which have been given letters of the Greek alphabet: Alpha,

Theta, Beta and Delta. The Delta state of meditation occurs when one is asleep, and the brain waves are rapid, from twenty-eight to thirty-five cycles per second.

The Gamma wave length is similar to the Delta, except that it occurs while you are wide awake and are conscious of everything that you are doing. In the Gamma state of meditation you achieve a suspended state of consciousness, where you are like a sleepwalker.

I learned this meditation from a famous Guru in India, who was one hundred and twenty-five years of age, and who was in remarkably good health. He had all his own teeth and hair, his eyesight was perfect and he had keen mental perception. He seemed to have the vitality of a man of forty.

This Guru called the Gamma wave length of meditation psychic somnambulism. It occurs when a person goes into a trance-like state and suspends his consciousness and lets a higher mind take over. The person appears to enter into a state of mental hibernation or sleep, with the eyes wide open.

Put yourself into the Gamma state of meditation by sitting quietly and looking at a spot above eye level on the opposite wall. Mentally go into a state of dream fantasy and project your mind into a world of spiritual reality, where you dream the things you desire into existence.

You create the mental and spiritual equivalents of the things you want and then project these dream patterns to the invisible cosmic protoplasm that fills the cosmos, creating there the imprints of what you want to occur in your life.

Within your consciousness you must create the dream that will one day clothe itself in objective reality and become the things you are dreaming into existence through the psychic somnambulism meditation.

Day dreams become reality when you learn how to release the psychic power of creativity through the following meditation:

> *I now enter into the state of psychic somnambulism, where I dream with my eyes wide open. I create the gamma state of meditation, where I am in spiritual ecstasy, attuned to the cosmic mind that knows all secrets and creates all things.*
>
> *I project now the psychic picture of my dream home, seeing it in all its reality. I mentally live in that dream home, entertain my friends there and walk through its rooms. I attend the garden of my dream home, gathering the fragrant flowers, and I sit*

before its fireplace on cold evenings, sharing my dream home with my friends and loved ones.

To make the dream home more concrete, before going into meditation, cut out pictures of actual houses and pick the one you want to meditate on. Or select portions of houses, and pictures of furnishings, and then in psychic somnambulism, walk through the house; furnish it, and entertain in it, until it becomes so real you know the location of every room.

Then meditate on your material abundance as follows:

I now meditate on attracting the perfect car that I desire. I project a Chevrolet (or meditate on any model or make of car you choose). I drive my car through the country. I project my friends and my family in it with me. I dream it into existence and I now claim it as my own.

I now project the sum of $5,000. which I wish to materialize for the purchasing of things I desire and for luxury and abundance. I now mentally bank this money. I go on a mental shopping spree, selecting objects I wish to buy.

5. For Releasing Creative Ideas and Inspiration

You can go into meditation and release creative ideas and inspiration for any purpose in life.

For this meditation go into the Alpha state and meditate as follows:

I am a creative center for great ideas. I now tap the hidden vein of gold within my subconscious mind and bring forth creative ideas for writing stories, composing songs, painting pictures, inventing objects, (here meditate on the specific field you are in for creative ideas in that field).

An architect who came to Hollywood, California from Atlanta, did this form of meditation and received inspiration to build a certain type of French Regency home for wealthy people in Beverly Hills and Bel-air, and he became rich through his creative ideas.

A chemist that came to my lectures learned about psychic somnambulism and in meditation received ideas for face creams and perfumes that he distributed through chains of department stores and he has made close to half a million dollars.

A salesman in real estate began using this form of meditation to increase his sales and he soon outsold all other salesmen in his office. He is now in his own firm and is one of the most successful younger real estate men in his region.

You can truly release miracle power when you use this form of meditation.

You can expand the meditation to fit other fields of endeavor, as follows:

> *I am a channel for creative ideas. I tap cosmic mind where all great thoughts are stored and I channel into my mind the illuminating ideas that great geniuses have used throughout the centuries.*
>
> *I am inspired by ideals of creative beauty and a desire to shape things of beauty for the good of the world.*

I knew an illustrator for children's stories who used this meditation for creating beauty and soon she had a job with one of the leading publishers of children's books, creating fantasy illustrations that delighted children.

6. For Physical Healing, Youth and Vitality

For achieving physical healing of the body and to release youthful energy and vitality for greater joy in living, go into the meditation known as the Alpha state, which brings your brain waves into the twelve to eighteen cycles per second range.

Meditate as follows, as you put yourself into a state of psychic somnambulism, in which you project the inner dream of health, youth and vitality from the subjective to the objective realm:

> *I project the dream of a perfect, healthy body. I know I am created in the image and likeness of God, therefore I know I am spiritual in nature. Spirit cannot be sick, grow old or die. I now create the dream of my soul's immortality and I become perfect, healthy and everlasting.*

How a Man Was Healed of Chronic Colds Through This Method

A man was chronically sick of colds that made him absent from work too many days each year. He was programmed to believe he had to catch colds. In winter it was due to the severe cold weather.

In summer it was a summer cold that took its toll. And in other seasons he laid it on to a virus or bug that was going around.

When he alkalinized his blood by using the above meditation, he also rid himself of colds forever. He dwelt on positive meditations rather than on the negative ones, and he was healed.

7. For Elevating the Consciousness to Superior Mental Action

You can build superior mental powers and literally achieve a high I.Q. that makes you a genius, if you meditate and build your mental level of efficiency even ten percent more than it is at the present time.

Go into the Theta state of meditation and think or say the following words, repeating them as often as you feel you need them:

> *I now slow down the rhythm of my brain and possess perfect control of all my faculties. I am able to concentrate on one thing at a time. I desire superior mental action where my mind will function with more efficiency and accuracy. I am now a channel for the cosmic mind to work through me. My superconscious mind now taps a strata of cosmic knowledge that has been re leased by geniuses throughout history. I wish to emulate their patterns of greatness and achieve outstanding success in my work.*

Take into your meditation sessions daily some of the great thoughts and inspirations of geniuses who have created magnificent works and be elevated in consciousness as you read or say their words, think their thoughts and attempt to reproduce their beauty.

This type of meditation on the thought forms of geniuses can extend to poetry, literature, music, science, invention, industry, exploration, philosophy and religion.

Someone said, "To be a Voltaire, think like a Voltaire."

Meditate on thoughts of greatness and riches and use specific examples to emulate and you will elevate your consciousness to superior mental action and become a creative genius.

How an Elevator Operator Became a Successful Businessman

I gave this meditation to one of my classes and a young man literally carried it into practice the next week. He was an elevator operator and told me before the class that he was limited in opportunities and income, but he longed to become something different.

He longed to get into the field of hair styling, where he could express his innate desire to create beauty for women. He had graduated from high school but could never go much higher than his present job.

In meditation this young man began to emulate thoughts of creative artists in his field. He meditated on the lives of people outstanding in the field of cosmetics, such as Helena Rubenstein, Elizabeth Arden, Max Factor, and Charles Revson of Revlon beauty products, until he was so enthusiastic that he was impelled by his intuitive mind to join a beauty college that gave night courses. He worked by day at his job, and studied at night. This young man became an outstanding hair stylist when he finished his course and later won every important national and international honor for his creative work in hair styling. Later he taught his system to advanced hair stylists, and was making fifty thousand dollars a year from his travels, exhibitions and teachings!

8. For Attracting Your Soul Mate
In Love and Marriage

In such a vitally important matter as love and marriage, you should never leave things to chance. Your conscious mind is often confused by surface appearances and you may be magnetically attracted to someone physically, only to find after marriage that the physical facade wears off and there is no true love to hold you together.

Meditation helps clear the consciousness in romantic matters and gives you true insight into the character and soul quality of the person you wish for your life mate.

Sit in meditation just before you go to sleep, and put yourself into the Delta state, where the brain waves become from twenty-eight to thirty-five cycles per second. As you lie there between sleeping and waking, create a state of fantasy in which you project the following meditation, with the thought of the qualities and appearance you want in your soul mate:

> *I desire completion in my love life. I ask my higher mind to intuitively guide me to my true soul mate. I want the following qualities in my mate: honesty. idealism, beauty of soul, kindness, consideration, loyalty and spirituality. I know there is a true soul mate that was created just for me and I now meditate on this perfect mate. As I drift off now onto the astral planes, my*

*soul shall seek and court my soul mate, for soul speaks to soul.
as star to star, and I know somewhere, waiting for me is my
perfect love.*

Then, as you drift off into sleep, your soul will receive its divine
impetus which will, like a compass, turn always to the North star of
divine romance.

How a Young Girl Found
Her Love through Meditation

A young girl of only eighteen was miserable at home, for her parents
were literally tyrants and demanded that she stay at home, insisting
she was too young to date. She learned about meditation and mystic
philosophy and she began to daily sit in meditation, where she fan-
tasized about her future lover.

Two months later she was sent by her parents to visit an aunt who
lived in Niagara Falls, to spend two or three weeks with her. This Aunt
was elderly and widowed and needed her companionship and assistance.
One day this girl was walking along the banks of the Falls, mixing
with the hundreds of tourists who were enjoying the scenery. Suddenly
someone bumped into her, and knocked her purse from her hands. She
reached down to pick it up and her head came to the same level as a
smiling, blue-eyed young man who hastily retrieved it and gave it back
to her. With profuse apologies for his carelessness, the young man asked
her if she had been hurt, and she laughingly replied she had not. The
young man fell into stride beside her, chatting casually about the
Falls, and asked her where she was from. She told him and he informed
her he lived in Toronto and was visiting friends in Niagara Falls. They
stopped and had lunch, and as the hour progressed this girl realized
here was the ideal soul mate she had been meditating on!

From this casual meeting, she later wrote me, developed a wonderful
romance. She was far enough away from her dominating parents to
avoid their interference, and they did not even know about it until
she wrote them that she was engaged to be married!

9. For Intuition and Psychic Phenomena

Elsewhere in this book we have explored methods for fully opening
the seventh chakra and discovering psychic powers. But there is a
special meditation which you can use that will aid you in this process.

The best state of meditation to go into for achieving psychic perception is the Alpha state. Your sense perceptions are all quickened by this form of meditation, and you will remove your own conscious, interfering mind, letting the higher intuitive and psychic centers give you guidance.

When you go into meditation for psychic guidance, you may take a piece of paper with you on which you write down some of the things you want to be guided in, such as: the choice of work, how to go into your own business, how to attract more money, where to find your true soul mate, whether you should buy or sell property or stocks at this time.

Then as you visualize the mental lake and see it perfectly still, meditate as follows:

> *I now ask the cosmic mind to guide me to the fulfillment of my destiny. I wish information and guidance on the following problems. (Here mentally consider each of your problems, letting your conscious mind present the problems to your higher, super-conscious mind. Then, let go of the problem, and give it to this higher mind with this statement.) I now release my problems into the loving care of the God mind, knowing that I shall be guided to take the right steps to fulfill my destiny.*

Then after meditation, go about your ordinary activities, confident that somehow, this higher mind will work out your problems perfectly.

10. For Cosmic Fulfillment and Spiritual Completion

In ancient Sanskrit the word Darshan means ultimate spiritual or cosmic fulfillment. In this state of consciousness your questing soul discovers the purpose back of life and you achieve peace of mind and peace of soul.

For this meditation go into the high vibrations of the Gamma state, where you reach a state of exhiliration and spiritual ecstasy. To help you achieve this, meditate on the opening of the petals of the sacred lotus blossom. Visualize your mind and soul as that sacred bloom, opening one petal at a time, revealing all the colors of the rainbow to your wondering gaze. For this meditation think or say the following words:

> *Ohm mane padme ohm, Ohm mane padme ohm. I now discover the jewel in the heart of the lotus. My soul now becomes*

the cosmic prism through which shines the pure white beam of God's infinite light, creating a kaleidoscope of all the colors of the rainbow. I am now bathed in consciousness by the Astral colors of rose, mauve, sunlight yellow, green, ethereal blue, and crimson red. As the sacred lotus now opens its beauteous petals I see revealed the distant vistas of the past. My soul traverses this mystical pathway to the light and I am enfolded by God's infinite beauty, surrounded by His infinite good, blessed by His infinite intelligence, and inspired by His infinite joy and Love. I am one with the light.

Review of Pointers in Chapter Twelve

1. How to achieve the ten states of positive meditation that make you a miracle worker, using supernormal powers to achieve your highest goals in life

2. How to attain memory retention and total recall of the past, through the brain wave state of meditation known as Theta.

3. A business executive used this meditation to overcome a poor memory and soon was able to retain thousands of new facts that helped his business.

4. How to use meditation for concentration, visualization and imagination, through the Alpha state and how it gives tremendous power to all departments of your life.

5. How to use the Beta state of meditation to help you solve problems through rationalization and reasoning.

6. A woman used this meditation to learn what she should do with a worthless piece of desert land. She was told to hold it and made $100,000 on the property!

7. How to use meditation to attract success and financial security through going into the Delta state.

8. How psychic somnambulism helps you create the destiny you want in the inner dream and then projects it to the outer world to make it a reality.

9. How to use meditation for releasing creative ideas and inspiration for anything you want to do in life, using the Alpha state for controlling your mind power.

10. How to release creative and inspiring ideas to your daily life bringing you tremendous subconscious mind power for achieving greatness and success.

11. How an architect, a chemist, and a real estate salesman all

used this meditation to create tremendous financial success in their respective fields.

12. How meditation can help you attain physical healing, youth and vitality by going into the Alpha state and releasing the natural healing agents of the brain and body.

13. A woman was healed of chronic colds through using this meditation.

14. How to elevate the consciousness to superior mental action by going into the Theta state of meditation and slowing down the rhythm of the brain for perfect control of all your faculties.

15. How an elevator operator became one of the country's leading hair stylists through using this meditation for achieving success.

16. How to use the right meditation to attract your true soul mate and find happiness in marriage. One young woman used this meditation to escape tyrannical parents and she found happiness in love.

17. How to attain Intuition and Psychic phenomena through meditation and be guided intuitively to do the right things in life.

18. The meditation to use for attaining cosmic fulfillment and spiritual completion, the state known as Darshan, in Sanskrit.

HOW TO PROJECT YOUR SOUL ON ASTRAL JOURNEYS THROUGH MYSTIC MEDITATION

13

From ancient India comes the mystical knowledge which can help you project your soul on astral journeys while you sleep. Transcendental meditation is used as the means for releasing the soul from the physical body and projecting it into the astral realms.

While you are out on the astral, your soul may acquire knowledge from ancient masters. You may become instructed in the arts, music, languages, history or the mystical secrets back of the cosmos. When you enter that mysterious forth dimensional world of spirit, you can tap unlimited powers and soar to mystic realms where the immortals dwell.

How a Guru of India Explained the Nature of the Soul

I once visited the Ashram of a famous Guru in India, and held many discussions with him about the nature of God, the soul, and the mysteries back of life. To illustrate the nature of the soul and why it is possible for it to go out on astral flights at night, he demonstrated something most interesting. He took a sponge and filled it with sand, then he immersed the sponge into a bucket of water. 'Now, you will notice," he said, "there are three substances here, each interpenetrating the other; the sponge, with sand inside of it, and water flowing through the sponge."

Then he took the sponge out of the water and pressing it between his hands he removed all the water. He then shook out the sand within the sponge. "Now, you will note," he said, "There are once again three separate substances. The sponge is analagous to the physical body of man. The sand is similar to man's brain, from which issues what we call mind. The water is similar to spirit or soul, which, when it is free of the sponge and the sand, returns once more to the sea, from whence it came. So too man's body contains a guiding agent, which is his brain, from which issues mind power, but the soul is a permeating, invisible intelligence which issues from God when we are born, and which, when we die, goes back to the source."

Then this Guru explained how through meditation just before going to sleep, we may send the soul out into the invisible, that it has a life of its own, and may explore the akashic record of the universe, on which is inscribed the entire history of the cosmos in invisible vibrations, which the soul may interpret.

AN ASTRAL JOURNEY TO ANCIENT TIBET

I went into meditation one night just before going to sleep and instructed my soul to go out into the astral and bring back knowledge I required for my lectures, when I was in world-famous Carnegie Hall.

I had what seemed like a vivid dream in which I seemed to be in an ancient land, in a monastery garden, with a group of yellow-robed monks. Then I became one of the monks, and went into a library lined with books, but they were not ordinary books as we know them. They were pieces of wood about ten inches long by six inches wide, on which were inscribed words in a strange language, which I easily understood. I studied these wooden tablets for some time and absorbed their meaning.

When this astral flight ended, I returned to my body and awakened, with a feeling that I was falling through space. I jotted down my impressions of what had occured on my astral flight and then went back to sleep again.

A few years later I picked up the New York *Times*, and on the front page of the second section, were photographs of wooden plaques that had been excavated in an ancient monastery in Tibet! The wooden tablets were the size and shape that I had seen in my astral journey and written in a strange language that was no longer in use.

THE METHOD TO USE TO PROJECT YOUR
SOUL ON ASTRAL JOURNEYS
THROUGH MYSTIC MEDITATION

1. To achieve astral projection, go into the meditation known as the Delta state. This is the rhythm of deep sleep and I have found that astral projection occurs best when the brain has reached this deep stage of meditation.

To achieve this Delta state of meditation breathe deeply ten or fifteen times. Then mentally project your mind back through time and space to the earliest days you can remember. Review the events of the past, fixing them in your mind and living through them as though they were projected on a motion picture screen in your mind.

2. When you have reached the deep stage of Delta meditation, and your brain rhythm has been accelerated, will your mind to project your soul back into time and space. Just as your mind has been able to recall memories on the akashic record of your brain, which are still real to you in memory recall, so too your soul can be willed to read the akashic record of the past, and fix in your mind the images of the historic march of events in the past.

3. Now when you have achieved this stage of meditation visualize your soul attached to your navel, just like the umbilical cord that tied you to your mother at time of birth.

4. Now meditate as follows, using these words, which you may memorize, or making up a similar dialogue which you hold with your soul, as you strive to project it out into the astral regions:

> *I now go into deep meditation, in which I wish to achieve astral projection. I wish to explore the akashic record of the past. I want to travel to ancient lands and times and be aware of the history of those days.*
>
> *I now command my soul to rise, achieving freedom from my physical body, and ascend into the astral realms. I wish to visit the ancient land of India, and explore the mysteries of that country. I wish to visit Egypt, in the early days of the Pyramids and know the mysteries in that ancient tomb of the Pharoahs. I wish to go to the mystical land of Tibet, beyond the ranges of the Himalaya mountains, and wander through its mystic bypaths, ac-*

cumulating sacred knowledge of the nature of the soul and the mystery called God.

My soul now ascends into the invisible, fourth-dimensional realm of spirit, and achieves freedom from the gravity pull of earth. Up—up—up, I rise, as my soul grows wings and achieves its liberation from the gravity pull of body and of earth.

5. When you reach this stage of your meditation, you should have a feeling of lightness in your body, and all physical sensations should end. You now become mind and spirit, liberated from the gross, physical body. You should have a feeling of rising in an airplane and you should experience a slight tugging sensation in the navel region, as you push up with your consciousness, attempting to liberate the soul from the gravity pull of the body.

6. At this stage of your meditation you may still have conscious awareness. You may feel you are rising, and be able to look back and see your physical body on the bed. You may be aware of the room, for it will seem to be lighted with a strange, phosphorescent glow, which is the aura that all physical substances give off. You may at this stage of meditation hear beautiful ethereal music, unlike anything heard from earthly instruments. You may see the flashing of colored lights, like a great cosmic rainbow, possessing a radiance and beauty that is celestial and unlike the colors perceived by your earthbound eyes.

How a Woman Used This Method
To Achieve Astral Projection

A lecture member in Los Angeles, who had learned how to go out into the astral, was a musician and composer. She achieved astral projection after trying three or four times, and at the moment of her soul's release she told me she heard the most beautiful music that no one on earth could possibly play. It was as if the celestical music of the spheres had been released from the combined beauty of the seas, mountains, trees, flowers, and earthly beauty, all creating a magnificent symphony that dazzled the senses.

From these astral flights this woman was able to bring back patterns of music that held her listeners enthralled, for she captured accurately many of the celestial sounds her soul had experienced in astral flight.

7. When you have achieved the first release of your soul in astral flight, you may direct it to any age or country you wish to visit. As there is no time or space but only spirit, in this vast cosmic domain of

the astral, you may have instantaneous flight from one century to another, or from one country to another. Spirit is analagous to light, which travels at the speed of 186,000 miles per second. Soul perception may embrace a hundred or a thousand years in a few seconds time, and perceive the pageant of history in a single second.

As a drowning man's entire life passes before his mind in a second, so too, in astral flight, you may have experiences that embrace several centuries. You have seen the delayed photographic process where a beautiful flower unfolds before your eyes from a bud into a full-blown blossom. You are witnessing there on the screen a process that took hours or days to achieve, but through the miracle of delayed photography, this process is accelerated into a few seconds time.

Your soul has this same identical ability, and may compress thousands of sights, sounds, colors and impressions that took months, years or even centuries to occur, into a brief span of time, which your questing soul may perceive in a few moments of astral flight.

How a Man Wrote An Historical
Novel Through Astral Flight

I knew a famous author who wrote historical novels, who practiced astral projection. He went back into the history of the period he wanted to write about, and on astral flights, he received characters, costumes, details of the history that no books could give him.

8. When you have once achieved astral projection and have had your journey into other dimensions of time, you may command your soul to interiorize in your body, by simply saying, "I want to go back to my earth body." Just as, when you are having a nightmare, you command yourself to awaken, so too you may come back at will from astral flights.

Do not fear that your soul cannot come back to your body, ror the cosmic time clock of your destiny is set and you cannot be locked into the cosmic wastelands by a freak accident. Your soul will return when your astral flight is finished, and you may go out as often as you wish on these astral journeys, and stay as long as you want to, and return safely to your body, without any danger or harm to yourself.

Review of Pointers in Chapter Thirteen

1. The mystical knowledge of how to project your soul on Astral journeys through transcendental knowledge that originated in ancient India.

2. How you may contact masters on astral planes and become instructed in art, music, languages, and learn mystical secrets from the fourth dimensional world of spirit.

3. The nature of the soul, the mystery of God and the purpose back of life, as explained by a Guru of India, in relation to meditation and astral projection.

4. How I once explored ancient Tibet on an astral journey and discovered wooden tables with sacred writings in a monastery garden.

5. How to go into the Delta state of meditation which is conducive to astral projection and release of the soul.

6. The meditation to use for achieving the exteriorization of the soul, and how to command the soul to leave the body.

7. The liberation of the soul from the body and how it is accompanied by sounds of celestial music and colors of the cosmic rainbow that are unbelieveable.

8. How a woman used this method to achieve astral projection and was able to tune in on celestial music that she brought back to enthrall her audiences in concert.

9. How illumined artists, composers, poets and dramatists have captured astral visions in their creations of art, music and literature.

10. How to select the age or country you wish to visit in astral flight, and perceive the pageant of history in a few moments time on the astral.

11. A man wrote an historical novel that was brought through while he was on astral flights to another age and country.

12. How to interiorize the soul back into the body from astral journeys, and achieve instant return without danger or fear of being locked into a cosmic wasteland.

HOW TO ENHANCE LOVE AND ATTRACT YOUR TRUE SOUL MATE THROUGH MEDITATION

14

Mystic philosophy reveals that love is the most creative power in the world. With love you can weave a spell about the hearts and minds of others and influence them to creative action. Through the bonds of love in marriage, you can create the miracle of life and have been given the Godly power to create in your image and likeness.

Through transcendental meditation you may achieve fulfillment of your destiny in love and marriage. You can send out the mystic design of love and it will weave a spell about the heart of your beloved and cause you to attract the one you love into your orbit of experience.

THE FOUR ASPECTS OF LOVE

There are four aspects of love and every person should experience all four, if he is to consider himself a completely integrated, happy person.

In this chapter we shall explore the method for using transcendental meditation to bring this divine emotion into focus in your life, so you can achieve benefits that transcend physical and material passion alone.

1. Procreative love.
2. Creative Love.

3. Love of Family.
4. Love of God.

How to Achieve The Four Aspects of Love with Meditation

1. Procreative Love.

The Bible gives us the principle that is back of all life and which is grounded in procreative love.

> Genesis 1: 27-28: *So God created man in his own image, in the image of God created he him; male and female created he them.*
> *And God blessed them, and God said unto them, be fruitful, and multiply, and replenish the earth, and subdue it: and have dominion over the fish of the sea, and over the fowl of the air. and over every living thing that moveth upon the earth.*

It is natural for you to want to marry and settle down and rear a family. But what happens in most cases where people marry? They do not meditate on the attraction of their ideal soul mate and they rush into a physical alliance, attracted by sexual magnetism alone. Then after a few months when this physical attraction wears off, they tire of each other and seek a divorce. It is tragic when a child is born of such a union for the ensuing separation creates problems for all concerned. Three out of five marriages in America end in the divorce courts.

How To Use Meditation To Attract Your True Soul Mate

To meditate on the ideal soul mate go into the meditation known as Beta.

As you sit in meditation visualize yourself climbing the spiritual mountain top, which helps elevate your consciousness above the physical and material realm.

Have an atmosphere that reflects peace, play some beautiful music of a romantic and tranquil type, such as Strauss waltzes, or Chopin's Polonaises. When you have achieved a sense of inner tranquility and your mind is cleared of all negativity and chaos, give yourself the following meditation, saying the words to yourself:

> *I now meditate on the highest ideals of love that I can enthrone in consciousness. I know that God is Love therefore love is the*

ultimate spiritual emotion that can bring about the unison of two souls in divine matrimony. I now ask divine guidance to the finding of my true soul mate. I desire marriage with the one person who possesses all the ideal qualities that I desire in my soul mate.

In this ideal union I shall express the qualities of cosmic love which are: a desire to share all experiences; mutual respect for one another; consideration for each other at all times; forgiveness of my mate's mistakes; appreciation of the others good qualities; tolerance of my mate's imperfections; The expression of kindness, and the giving of praise when it is deserved. I shall daily express the divine emotion of love, compassion, understanding and forgiveness.

When you have attuned your higher mind centers by using this meditation, you will have so magnetized your mind that you will automatically vibrate only to the qualities you have expressed in meditation. When you meet members of the opposite sex, you will instantly be guided by your higher psychic centers to the persons who radiate the qualities you have imprinted on your higher mind centers.

How a Twenty-five Year Old Woman Attracted True Love

A woman in my lecture work told me she felt she would become an old maid, because she could never find a man who measured up to her ideals. She was twenty-five and said, "Where can I ever meet a man who will make a perfect husband and be a good father to my future family? Most men are interested in only the physical emotions now-a-days."

I instantly changed her thinking and told her how she should go into meditation and charge the magnetic centers of her consciousness with the ideal soul mate she wanted to attract. She was searching for her marriage partner with the usual woman's conscious mind and it had failed her.

This woman went into daily meditation and said the above meditation for a period of three weeks. She stopped her frantic worrying and searching and put the problem into the hands of a cosmic intelligence which knew where her soul mate was.

One night she went to a party being given by a nurse of her aquaintance. Half an hour later she was dancing with a tall, good-looking, dark-haired young man who worked as an intern in a hospital. He was studying to become a pediatrician, and this girl felt psychically that here was the ideal man she had waited for all her life. They both loved children. He was highly idealistic and so devoted to his work that he did not play around like most of his friends did.

The intern asked her if he might call her some time, and took her telephone number. She thought pessimistically, "That's the last I'll hear of him!" The following week on Saturday, he called and asked her for a date. She told me later that they were compatible from the moment they met. They liked the same music, the same foods, the same TV programs. He had been waiting for his soul mate all his life, and he proposed marriage within three months time!

2. Creative love

Every person should have creative love in his life. The limitations of procreative love are evident. We can have children and rear them successfully, but when that task is finished for a woman, at approximately forty or forty-five, shall she be finished with life and with love.?

It is obvious that it was God's intention to channel tremendous creative power through the love urge when it is elevated to its proper plane of creative action.

Most of the world's great art, music, poetry, literature, science, inventions and industrial achievements were created because of the inspirational power of love.

Back of every successful man, it is said, there is the love of a woman. Statues are reared to Lincoln, Washington, Pasteur and Columbus, but what of the invisible memorials created by their loving mothers, sweethearts and wives?

See the enduring and beneficial effects of love in the lives of such great souls as Florence Nightingale, who elevated the profession of nursing to new heights. Witness the heroic proportions of love that Father Damien had for the lepers at Molokai, when he labored among them and gave his life in their service.

Creative love is the dynamic power back of magnificent music. More songs have been written about love than about any other subject. More poems and stories and dramas have been fashioned about this subject than any other. Creative love must be expressed by every living human being, if he wishes to elevate labor into an inspirational force for the good of humanity.

Meditation for achieving creative love

Go into the stillness and visualize the spiritual lake, putting yourself into the Alpha state of meditation.

Say or think the following meditation:

> *I now meditate on the second facet of divine love. I express the creative urge for the good of humanity. I am now in the flow of inspirational ideas and creative energy. I channel this creative love to my daily tasks. I lovingly serve in my work, knowing that I am transmitting my ideas, service and labor into the enduring fabric of my destiny.*
>
> *I elevate my consciousness to high levels of inspiration through love. I feel this divine emotion in all my relations with people with whom I work. I draw upon the inspiration of my higher consciousness and bring it to my daily tasks, making them joyous, constructive and loving.*

A schoolteacher's experience

A school teacher I know uses this meditation each day before going to her work, and she tells me that it makes her tasks more enjoyable than formerly.

A court judge's experience

I knew a judge in superior court in Los Angeles who had studied metaphysics with me years before, and he told me that whenever he faced an especially difficult day in his court, he would clear his consciousness first with this meditation. He said that power and endurance came from some higher source, and he felt he could dispense justice with greater integrity because of his meditations.

3. Love of family

The emotion of love is most naturally expressed in relation to one's own family first, for blood ties are the closest we may know in our human relationships.

Many families express love occasionally but there are long periods of time in between where they sometimes are inclined to be cross and intolerant.

I once knew a man who was an excellent provider for his family of two children, but when he had an argument with his wife, he would go for days without speaking to either the wife or children! These spells of hatred and anger cancelled out all the love and protection he furnished his family when he was in a happy mood. His children grew up lacking in respect for their father, and the mother died at an early age. One of the daughters told me she felt it was because of the father's frequent anger and neglect. The father no doubt felt guilt at the way he had treated his wife while she lived.

To keep yourself attuned to divine love in relation to your family members use the following meditation:

> *I am now in tune with divine love on all planes. I generate love and kindness this day that I shall express all day to members of my family. If there is anyone I have mistreated or unjustly accused, I now forgive them and ask their forgiveness for my conduct. I am now in joyous bonds of accord and harmony with all my family and express my gratitude to them for their many kindnesses, and my appreciation for their love and kindness.*

How a Woman Was Healed Through This Meditation of Love

A woman I knew, who came into our lecture work in New York City, had hated her sister for twenty years. They had a disagreement over the father's will and one had received more than the other in the settlement. This led to unjust accusations and hatred on both sides.

This woman developed a severe bronchial affliction and had pneumonia twice in ten years. When she came into our work, she was feeling pains from arthritis, and changed her diet often, but to no avail. When she told me her twenty-year burden of hatred, I knew why she was sick. I gave her this meditation for love, and urged her to write her sister, asking her forgiveness. The sisters reconciled and lived together happily after that. They both began coming to my lectures, and the sister that was sick had a complete healing within three months time!

The fruits of hate

Very often we keep our good from us by expressing the negative emotion of hatred. Another instance I knew where love turned to hate was of a girl who was very close to her father. She adored him, and he lavished so much love on her that it often caused friction between him and his wife. His wife died and he was left alone with his adoring daughter. But the father was still vigorous and felt the need of a wife's love, so he married again. His daughter hated her step-mother and moved out of the house.

When I met her in New York she told me of her dislike of the step-mother, and how she had become estranged from her father. "He should not have married again," she lamented, "Out of respect for my mother." She selfishly wanted her father to spend his declining years alone, with only her love to sustain him.

I pointed out to her that this was wrong and selfish and urged her to make up with her father and step-mother. She paid them a visit in a mid-western town that summer, when she had her vacation. Her father had become quite wealthy through real estate speculation over the years. Now he was a semi-invalid, owing to an injury he had sustained, and his wife took splendid care of him.

Two years later the father died, and when the will was read, he had left his wife half of his estate and the rest to his daughter. In a letter he left with the lawyers, the father explained how, out of anger, he had cut his daughter off completely in his original will, but had changed it two years before when she reconciled with him! That expression of family love repaid this girl with a $50,000 inheritance!

4. Love of God

The most vital facet of the cosmic diamond of love is the expression of that divine emotion in our love of God, the creator.

Many times people who have expressed love on all other planes, leave out this vital element from their blueprint of destiny. They rear their families, their mates die and they grow old, feeling that now there is nothing more for them to look forward to. Many times such people have had happy marriages, have reared successful families, and they sit back and await the end of life in loneliness and with feelings of frustration.

It is at such times of bitterness and defeat that we need the sustaining power of love of God.

This divine emotion should be felt every day of our lives, not only when we have reached the sunset years and are preparing for the transition called death. Man's soul should be in divine communion with this most holy of all emotions, the love of God, every day of his life.

To instill this greatest of all emotions in your heart and soul, begin each day of your life when you awaken, with this meditation on the love of God.

I now thank God for another glorious day of life. I awaken to the divine emotion of Love for God and all humanity. I now dedicate my breath this entire day as a song of thanksgiving to the creator of the universe, and every time I breathe today, it shall be a song celestial, rising to the cosmic heights, in perpetual praise and glory to the Father of all creation.

Meditation from a Tibetan Monk

I once met a Tibetan monk in the north of India, and we walked together in a secluded monastery, from which, in the distance, we could see the towering sacred ranges of the Himalayas, beyond which was his retreat.

This Monk carried a miniature prayer wheel, on which were attached colored bits of paper. He explained to me: "On these pieces of paper are written prayers, and every time I turn the prayer wheel these hundreds of prayers ascend to the Celestial heights in perpetual praise of God. In the Monastery at Lahasa, we have a prayer wheel with a thousand prayers on it, and each day the monks turn this wheel, putting us in constant communication with God, the source of all life and love." Then he told me how we, in the western world, may utilize the same principle of Holy Meditation by dedicating every breath to God for the entire day, when we first awaken in the morning.

Review of Pointers In Chapter Fourteen

1. How the emotion of love can be used to weave a mystic spell about the hearts and minds of others, and to influence them to creative action.

2. The four aspects of love that every person should utilize if he wishes to have a balanced, well-integrated and happy life experience.

3. How procreative love is the principle back of all life and must be invoked to multiply and replenish the earth.

4. How you can use meditation to attract your true soul mate, and help elevate your consciousness above the physical and material plane of love and passion.

5. How a twenty-five-year old woman, who thought she would always be an old maid, used this meditation to attract a young intern, who was her true soul mate in every respect.

6. How creative love works to channel tremendous creative power for great art, music, literature, science, invention and industry. Back of every successful man is a woman's love.

7. How a school teacher, and a judge, each used this meditation for creative love, each day to help make their work more joyous and productive.

8. How the love of family is another facet of the cosmic diamond of love and produces unity, harmony and joy in life.

9. How a man violated this law of love and suffered guilt, misery and lost the respect and love of his wife and two daughters.

10. How a woman used this meditation of love to overcome hatred she had held for her sister over twenty years, and was cured of bronchial ailment and arthritis.

11. A young woman forgave her father for an alleged mistake he had made when he married another woman, and through extending love and understanding once again, she inherited the sum of $50,000. when the father died.

12. Love of God, the most vital facet of the cosmic diamond of love and how it sustains humanity in time of need.

13. Secret meditation obtained from a Tibetan Monk near the Himalayas, in which the power of God is invoked every day with every inhalation of breath, releasing tremendous physical, material and spiritual power.

HOW TO USE THE SACRED FLAME MEDITATION FROM THE TEMPLE OF ISIS FOR SUPERNORMAL POWERS

15

One of the most potent forms of meditation is that which is invoked through the sacred flame ritual from the Temples of Isis and Osiris in the Pyramid of Gizeh, in Egypt.

For centuries, the ancient Egyptians knew that there was some higher power which could be released in the human psyche through invocation and ritual.

In this ancient system, meditation was used as the means for suspending the conscious mind and opening the higher centers of consciousness. In this way the full force of man's higher psychic centers was put into action, and he could literally perform miracles of faith in every department of his life.

THE MIRACLES YOU CAN PERFORM THROUGH THE SACRED FLAME MEDITATION

1. You can use the sacred flame ritual to solve problems and overcome the daily challenges that rise.
2. You can put into the sacred flame your dreams and aspirations, writing them down fully, and then consigning them

to the flame, releasing the creative spirit that will manifest whatever you have written down.

3. You can raise the level of your inspiration to new heights for any creative endeavor you wish to perform, such as writing stories, painting pictures, inventing new objects, composing beautiful music, or going into a new business venture.

4. You can invoke the magnetic power of love and work the magic of attraction in the heart of the person you wish to attract.

5. You can use the sacred flame ritual to remove obstacles, persons, and unpleasant conditions from your environment.

6. You can perform the miracle of healing sick bodies; yours, or your friends and relatives, by invoking the healing arts of the cosmic mind.

7. With the sacred flame ritual you can banish poverty and hardship and attract a new job, more money, and financial security for your family and yourself.

8. You may also use the sacred flame ritual for other than physical and material benefits; you may use it to elevate your consciousness to an expanded spiritual awareness that gives you peace of mind and greater faith in God

THE MIRACLE POWER OF FAITH
AND HOW IT WORKS

At the basis of the sacred flame ritual from the Temples of Isis and Osiris, is the miracle power of faith. This miracle power was invoked by the Master Jesus each time He achieved a healing. He said, "Thy faith hath made thee whole." (Matthew 9:22). "If thou canst believe. All things are possible to him that believeth."

"I will restore health unto thee, and I will heal thee of thy wounds, saith the Lord." (Jeremiah 30:17)

The power of your higher spiritual self is released when you believe in miracles. The magic power of faith helps trigger the autonomic nervous system that controls the glands, the heart and lungs.

We are told, "Faith without works is dead." (James 2:26) When you use the sacred flame ritual and go into meditation, with faith, you will begin to see the results of faith in your business affairs, in your body, in your environment and in the peace and security that you will experience in mind, body and soul.

THE REGIME FOR USING THE SACRED FLAME
RITUAL MEDITATION

1. Create a sacred shrine before which you will meditate, when you wish to invoke the sacred flame ritual. Have a small urn in which you can burn a piece of paper. Have a series of different colored candles which you will use for different meditations. Put up an emblem, a cross or some sacred relic of your particular faith. If you can find an Egyptian reproduction of some small article from the Pyramids it will help focus your higher mental powers.

2. Have the room in which you will perform the sacred flame ritual dark, with only the light of the candle and, later, when you burn the paper, the light from the flame. You may perform the sacred flame ritual alone or have close friends or relatives perform it with you. However, be certain that they come to this sacred ritual with faith, for one unbeliever can create an atmosphere of disbelief that cancels out the positive concentration of other minds.

3. You may have soft, peaceful music playing in the background. The composition, "Meditation," from *Thais,* is excellent for this purpose. Also, "In A Monastery Garden."

4. You may sit in a comfortable position before the altar you have created, with the candle on a table near the urn, in which you will burn the paper. Have a pen and pieces of blank paper handy, on which will be written your requests for burning in the sacred flame.

5. Before starting the meditation on the sacred flame, write down your requests on pieces of paper. Make these small in size and use two or three, putting down as many requests as you desire. There is no limit to the power you will invoke; the only limit is your faith or lack of it. If you write down that you want a million dollars, with tongue in cheek, saying to yourself, "I know this is ridiculous but let's see what will happen." You will automatically negate the power that you wish to invoke. If you write down $1,000 and really believe it is possible to achieve that sum within a certain period of time, you will have an excellent chance of obtaining it.

How a Woman Demonstrated $5,000
through the Flame Ritual

A woman in Los Angeles, who began to use this sacred flame ritual had many small demonstrations right from the beginning. She had a wart on her face that she wanted removed, and after invoking the power through the sacred flame, it disappeared within one month. Then she asked for a trip to Hawaii on a second honeymoon, to win back her husband's waning love. That year he obtained a bonus on a big account he won for his firm, and they took the honeymoon cruise and she won back his love. Her third attempt was to ask for $5,000 to help remodel a home for her married son and his family. This seemed impossible of attainment. She set the time limit to six months. Within three months time it came about in the most unusual manner. Her husband had bought some cheap mining stock in Canada years before and put the certificates in a trunk and forgot about it. The company seemed to have gone broke, but someone had bought up the stock, refinanced the company again, and one day she read in the papers that the stock was now worth $5,000 more than they had paid for it! She got the exact amount she had put into the sacred flame ritual meditation!

6. You may use the following wording on your slips of paper, or make up your own to fit your exact needs. Keep the wording brief and to the point. Your higher psychic centers know your needs and you need only project these briefly in writing, to focus them more clearly in your higher mind centers.

A. To Solve Problems And Overcome Challenges

Write on your slip or slips of paper one or more problems. My problem is:

> Trouble at my work.
> Family friction and discord.
> Lack of money.
> Physical sickness.
> Worry and anxiety.
> Romantic problems.
> Bad habit of smoking, or drinking, or gambling.
> Lack of memory.

B. To Manifest Your Dreams And Aspirations

I desire the following:

> The sum of $1,000 within three months.
> A new job in work that I enjoy.
> A house of my own, or an apartment I like.
> A trip to Europe on my vacation.

To marry my true soul mate.
An interesting social life.
A healing of my body.
A good memory and better intellect.

A woman in our lecture work in New York city, tried the sacred flame meditation and wrote down three things in this list: A home of her own. An interesting social life and marriage with her true soul mate. She had perfect faith that she would have all three within the year's time limit she set.

She worked for a big legal firm and made a good salary but lived in a small apartment. She projected the perfect dream home, and one day a wealthy woman client of one of the attorneys in her office, asked her if she knew anyone who would care to share her big home in New Jersey with her for a reasonable rent. She was divorced and the big house was lonely and too expensive for her. The girl looked at the house and it was ideal. It was spacious, with a large garden, and her own private apartment, bath and kitchen! She moved in at once, and part of her dream was fulfilled.

The biggest miracle was still to occur. The second half of her request was instantly filled, for this woman had very interesting friends and when they visited the house she introduced them to the young secretary and she had a wonderful new social life without making any effort. When she wondered how the third miracle would occur, the higher powers were already at working fashioning the tapestry of dreams she had projected in the sacred flame ritual. One night at one of the social gatherings at the house, a young attorney visited, with a young woman, whom the secretary thought was his wife. It turned out that the attorney was a bachelor and he could hardly keep his eyes from courting the secretary all evening. She felt certain that this was the true soul mate she had projected in the sacred flame ritual.

The following day this young attorney called her at the office and asked her for a date. He explained that the girl with him the night before was only a casual acquaintance. Within six months this young lady was on her honeymoon to Europe...a secret desire she had long held, but had been afraid to put into the sacred flame ritual!

C. To Raise Inspiration For Creative Work

I wish this creative gift:

To write stories.

To paint pictures.
To invent objects.
To compose music.
To go into business.

Write down only a short sentence on the piece of paper you will consign to the sacred flame, for your higher mind knows the nature of your request.

You can put any kind of creative gift you wish to attain. You may put down some special quality of mind you want to develop, or you may write down that you want a magnetic and charming personality.

You may also write down one or more of these special creative gifts. The only limitation there is to this power is your own lack of faith. If you believe in it, you are on the way to achieving the gift you ask for.

D. To Invoke The Magnetic Power of Love

I wish to attract my true soul mate.
I desire marriage with (write name of person here)
I wish to arouse love in (write person's name)
I wish to re-kindle love in my mate.
To remove obstacles in love, (or marriage).
I wish to become more magnetic in love.

Whatever situation you wish to create in love or marriage write it down briefly on the piece of paper, using the name of the person you wish to attract or influence in love or marriage.

How a Man Overcame Insuperable Odds in Love

A young man of twenty-four came from a very wealthy family and had a sincere desire to marry a girl whose family was poor and socially unimportant. The boy's family had already planned marriage with a girl who was socially prominent and belonged to the same social set. The father threatened to cut the boy off in his will if he married the girl of his choice.

When the young man sought me out for counsel, he was in a terrible state of mind. "I love Linda," he told me, "and I want to marry her, but how can I go ahead and hurt my family, especially my father, who wants me to marry someone else?"

Although the young man was graduated from Yale, and the last person in the world you'd think would believe in mystic rituals from ancient temples, I was surprised to find he already knew of the Alpna brain wave miracles being performed in the medical schools of the country's leading universities. He had heard of the flame ritual in connection with removing warts and dissolving tumors by burning their facsimilies on pieces of paper, with the recitation of certain invocations. He did not know about the ritual originating in the Temples of Isis and Osiris, however, so I quickly gave him a sketch of the background of this powerful meditation.

I then told him to write down on a piece of paper the following requests:

I wish to marry Linda, my true soul mate.
I wish to remove all obstacles to our love.

Then, burning the white candle, I gave the sacred invocation with him, as we consigned the piece of paper, with his name on it, in the urn, while I said the ancient invocation.

He thanked me and left, promising to keep me advised as to the outcome of his romance with Linda.

My answer came just two months later, in the form of an engraved wedding invitation to their wedding, which was being held in one of the most beautiful cathedrals in New York City! It was after the wedding, at the reception, that he told me, his face alight with joy, how the miracle had occurred.

"Two weeks after we had our interview my father came down with a mild heart attack, his second in five years. At the hospital he took my hand in his and said, 'I was wrong in objecting to your marriage to Linda, son. Life is short, and if you two kids love each other, you have my blessings to get married.'"

The father was at the wedding, and I have never seen a prouder or more healthy man. I believe he had his healing through that wise decision.

E. To Remove Obstacles, Undesirable Persons and Unpleasant Conditions From Your Environment

I wish to overcome enmity in my work.
I wish to change environment in my office or home.
I wish to remove interference of (name of person.)
I wish to remove animosity of (name of person.)
My parents objections to my way of life.

Choose whatever obstruction is in your path to the achievement of your desired goal and put it down on a slip of paper. Do not project harm or injury to any person, for this negative force is called black magic and works against you. The Sacred Flame Ritual is a positive form of white magic and is to be used only for good purposes. If it is used for evil, even to try to destroy evil, it is apt to short circuit your positive forces and do harm, so always avoid naming any person you wish removed through accident, sickness or death.

Instance of How Black Magic Worked Harm

A woman used black magic to try and get rid of her rival for her husband's love. She was told to get a small doll and put pins into the body, projecting the thought that her rival would be destroyed. Three weeks after this ritual, this woman who had put the pins in the doll, began to feel pains in her chest region. She was rushed to the hospital for an emergency gall bladder operation that nearly killed her!

When you invoke the power of the sacred flame ritual, do not try to play God. Leave it up to the higher powers to dispense divine justice. The method for doing this is something you cannot select. The evil forces are always brought down, and the good forces are always rewarded by the great law of Karma. All you need do is invoke the power to bring this cosmic power into perfect balance in your own life.

F. To Perform Miracles of Healing

I wish to remove this physical infirmity. (It is not necessary to name the condition, for your higher mind knows what condition you are trying to cure.)

> *I wish to achieve perfect healing of my body.*
> *I wish to have more energy and youthful vitality.*
> *I wish to regulate my heartbeat and blood pressure so they are perfect.*

When you enter into the state of meditation for healing and write down the condition you wish removed, have faith that the higher cosmic mind knows how to heal you and believe that the miracle begins to work the moment you consign the paper to the sacred flame.

G. To Attract More Money and Financial Security

> I desire more money from my work.
> I wish to have a change of job.

I wish a promotion in my work.
I desire the sum of $1,000 within three months.
I wish a new car.

A woman burned the paper in the sacred flame ritual on which she had written "I wish a promotion in my work." She had also written that she wanted the sum of $500 from unexpected sources. Within one month from the time she began her invocation, she was given a promotion as office manager, with a raise in salary of approximately $500 a year!

One young lady working for the same firm for five years had not had a raise in salary for a long time. She invoked the sacred flame ritual, asking for a raise of ten dollars a week. One day her boss called her into his office and, like a man in a trance, he gave her the exact raise she had asked for.

H. To Achieve Spiritual Awareness and Peace of Mind

I desire higher spiritual awareness.
I wish to know the mystery of the soul.
I desire to come closer to God.
I wish to channel infinite intelligence.
I wish for peace of mind and peace of soul.

When you meditate on spiritual awareness you are asking the higher powers for omniscience, to know all; omnipotence, to be all powerful spiritually and omnipresence, the finding of God everywhere, in all creation and tapping this higher power in your daily life.

How To Perform The Sacred Flame Ritual Meditation

When you have determined the things you wish to ask in the sacred flame ritual, and have prepared the piece or pieces of paper, with your requests briefly listed, you may then approach the shrine, light a white candle, and stand before the altar, with the pieces of paper in your hand.

You may then read the following invocation to the Sacred Flame, which comes from the inscriptions found on the walls of the Temples of Isis and Osiris. In ancient Egypt, a High Priestess did the ceremony in the temple of Isis, which was the lesser light, signified by the moon. Osiris was the greater light or flame, signified by the sun. The body of Osiris was symbolically cut up and burned in the sacred flame as the ritual was intoned by the High Priestess.

The four elements of creation are involved in this ritual of fulfillment. Air is the creative element of mind. Water, is the spiritual element of soul. Earth is the physical element of creation, in which we have our being. Fire is the purifying and creative spirit which burns away the dross of material substance, leaving the pure gold of spirit or soul.

The Sacred Flame Meditation For Supernormal Powers

I now approach the sacred shrine, in the Temple of Isis, to ask for assistance of the higher spiritual forces. I now consign to the sacred flame these dreams, aspirations and desires, inscribed on these pieces of paper, asking that they be manifested through creative spirit. (Now light one of the slips of paper and drop it into the urn, and as you continue the balance of the invocation, put the other pieces of paper into the urn, letting them also catch· fire.)

I now release the creative power of the sacred flame that will burn away all obstacles and obstructions that stand in the path of my achieving my objectives in life. My dreams and desires are now released as pure flame, creative spirit, and as these requests ascend to the illimitable spiritual heights, they will clothe themselves in their physical and material counterparts, manifesting on earth the images that are inscribed hereon.

Ashes to ashes and dust to dust. Now all physical obstructions are removed and in the clear, purifying flame of Osiris, the golden Sun, these dreams ascend heavenward, where they find their true fulfillment in reality.

I now have faith that these desires shall be transmitted to the objective realm of reality, from the dream world of spirit. I expectantly await my good knowing that it is rushing forth to meet me and fulfill my destiny.

When the flame has completely died out and only charred ashes remain, crumble them up and remove them to be disposed of. You may perform this ritual for as many different things as you wish to materialize. It should not be done again after the first time, for at least two or three more weeks, giving the mystical forces time to bring your desires into manifestation. Sometimes the power works at once, and sometimes it takes longer, depending on your faith and the nature of your requests.

COLORED CANDLES TO BE USED
FOR VARIOUS PURPOSES

You may perform the Egyptian Sacred Flame Ritual using various colored candles for various purposes.

Use the *white* candle for general purposes, as white is the highest spiritual color, containing all colors.

Use *rose* for invoking high creative and inspirational power for writing, composing, painting, or evolving other talents.

Use a *blue* candle for friendship, love and releasing emotional power.

Use a *red* candle for healing the body of sickness.

Use a *yellow* candle for materializing money or other material substance or objects.

Use a *black* candle for removing unpleasant conditions and obstructions that stand in the way of your achievement. Also, when you wish to remove some objectionable person from your environment, the black candle should be burned.

Use a *green* candle when you wish to find something you have lost or to succeed in investments such as stocks, gold mining, oil drilling, uranium or other precious metals.

Review of Pointers in Chapter Fifteen

1. The Sacred Flame Ritual from the Temples of Isis and Osiris in the Pyramid of Gizeh, and how it can be used to invoke high spiritual powers.
2. The eight miracles you can perform through using the sacred flame ritual, and how to utilize it to invoke supernormal mental and spiritual powers.
3. The miracle power of faith invoked by the Master Jesus and how the sacred flame ritual also works through faith.
4. How to create a special shrine with colored candles before which you can invoke the sacred flame meditation.
5. How one woman used the sacred flame ritual to materialize

$5,000 from unexpected sources. She also had two other amazing miracles that brought her great joy.

6. The meditation to use for solving problems and overcoming challenges of life, lack of money, sickness, worry and anxiety and bad habits, such as smoking.
7. How to use the sacred flame ritual to raise high inspiration for creative work, for writing, painting, inventing, composing and similar talents.
8. How to use the sacred flame ritual to manifest your dreams and aspirations, to find new job, to attract your own home, and to achieve fulfillment.
9. How one woman achieved three of her big dreams through the sacred flame ritual, including marriage with a perfect soul mate.
10. How to invoke the magnetic power of love through using the sacred flame ritual, and achieving fulfillment in love and marriage.
11. How a young man won his love against the opposition of his family, by using the sacred flame ritual for finding love fulfillment.
12. How you can use the sacred flame ritual to remove obstacles, undesireable persons and unpleasant conditions from your environment.
13. How a woman wrongly used black magic to rid herself of a rival for her husband's love and was nearly destroyed.
14. How to perform miracles of healing through the sacred flame ritual, for regulating the body's automatic functions and releasing the healing power.
15. How to use the magic power of the sacred flame ritual to attract more money and achieve financial security, to change jobs, win promotions in work, and specific sums of money.
16. How to perform the sacred flame ritual, releasing the higher power of the psycho-neuro centers of consciousness and enlisting the aid of higher spiritual forces in the universe.

THE GOLDEN KEYS OF MEDITATION THAT OPEN MYSTIC DOORS TO COSMIC CONSCIOUSNESS

16

Throughout the centuries there have been illumined souls who have been able to probe secrets of the universe and bring to humanity brilliant ideas that have advanced civilization to great heights of achievement.

These illumined souls we call geniuses. In reality, however, these great men and women did not possess extraordinary minds. They used their mind power differently from ordinary mortals. These great souls used the power of meditation to open mystic doors to cosmic consciousness. They performed their seeming miracles because they tapped a strata of mental and spiritual power which caused them to become geniuses.

No matter with what limitations you were born, if you possess an innate desire to elevate yourself, to expand your consciousness you may achieve the great heights that these geniuses attained.

In this chapter we shall discover the golden keys of transcendental meditation which you may use to open the mystic doors to cosmic consciousness. Your life will change, as if by a miracle, when you utilize this dynamic power of meditation.

COSMIC CONSCIOUSNESS

There are certain distinguishing signs that mark those who have attained cosmic consciousness. When you once go into meditation to achieve this state of expanded consciousness, you will see if these signs appear in your life.

Cosmic consciousness gives you a *sense of instant perception*, that might almost be called psychic or clairvoyant. You will know something without knowing how you know. You will go into meditation and probe a mystery, then all of a sudden you will become one with the mystery and you will be aware of the most profound and complicated secrets of the universe.

THROUGH MEDITATION THE SECRET
OF GRAVITY WAS REVEALED

When Newton sat one day under an apple tree, in deep meditation on the mystery of life, he saw the first sliver of a new moon in the blue skies. At the same time an apple fell to earth, and in a moment of great apperception Newton thought: "The moon in the heavens, and the apple on earth, are both falling through space. The same identical power motivates the moon and the apple." Thus, in that moment of cosmic awareness was born his third law of motion and the law of magnetic attraction known as gravity.

GREAT MUSIC WAS COMPOSED
THROUGH COSMIC CONSCIOUSNESS

To show you how this mystical power works to bring cosmic consciousness, an illustration from history will reveal how a great composer, Beethoven, achieved some of his great works. One night Beethoven was walking on a clear, cold winter night in Munich where he was giving a concert on the following evening. Suddenly he heard someone trying to play his beautiful Sonata in F Major but doing a very bad job of it. Then he heard a girl say in a despairing voice, as she suddenly stopped playing, "Oh, I can never do it justice! It is too beautiful!"

The Master climbed the short flight of stairs to the apartment from which he had heard the music and knocked on the door. It was opened by a young man, who admitted the composer. Sitting at the piano was a blind girl, the young man's sister. Beethoven explained that he had heard her futile attempt to play the composition and he sat down at the piano and said, "Permit me to play it for you." At the sound of the first golden notes that issued from the piano, the blind girl recognized the touch of the Master, Beethoven himself. She sat spellbound while the great composer finished the composition. Then, as the silvery moonlight cascaded through the windows, making mystic patterns on the floor, and the soft, white mantle of snow shrouded the earth, the icicles glistened like diamonds on the trees outside the window, as a full moon rode high in the heavens. Beethoven's fingers wandered idly over the keyboard, as he sat there in deep meditation, enchanted by the mystic beauty of the night, he said, "I shall compose a sonata to the moonlight." He began to play a hauntingly lovely refrain that held his listeners transfixed; then, when he had finished he gave the young couple tickets to his concert the next night, and rushed home to spend the rest of the night writing down the beautiful "Moonlight Sonata," which has enchanted millions over the years.

Such is the creative power of meditation; when the mind is elevated to inspirational heights cosmic consciousness is awakened and the creative power of a genius will rush forth to perform some astounding miracle.

THE FIVE GOLDEN KEYS
TO MYSTIC MEDITATION

1. A desire to create something beautiful and enduring for the world.
2. The emotion of love, when it is elevated to its highest plateau of creative action.
3. A desire to share your good with others, through charitable impulses.
4. The master motive to create prosperity, happiness and peace for all humanity.
5 A desire to know God, to love Him, and bring His divine laws into expression.

These five golden keys to mystic meditation help focus cosmic mind power in your own higher brain centers. Cosmic consciousness awakens in the minds of those who wish to become channels for God to express Himself through. All great geniuses in art, music, literature, science and industry, have been motivated by a desire to educate others, to refine and perfect their talents, so they can help others. They have all tapped cosmic consciousness with their desires to uplift, inspire, elevate and transform humanity.

**The Regimen For Using the Golden
Keys of Meditation That Open Doors
to Cosmic Consciousness**

    **1. A desire to create something beautiful
    and enduring for the world**

When you use this golden key of meditation, go into the stillness and create the Alpha state of meditation, where your mind is still and peaceful as a lake. Then consciously bring into focus on the screen of your mind the most beautiful things that you can remember. Recall the magnificent scenes you have looked upon since earliest childhood of mountains, rivers and peaceful valleys. Review all the beautiful sunrises or sunsets you have seen, with their incandescent molten gold and crimson flame splashed upon the panorama of skies and oceans and landscapes.

Visualize the beauty of the sacred lotus blossom as you sit in deep meditation, striving to capture its purity and its symbolical meaning. When you seek inspiration for creating something beautiful and enduring for the world, this meditation should be used, saying the words to yourself or thinking them:

> *I now enter the alpha state of meditation wherein my mind becomes as peaceful and still as a lake. Now, like a mirror, my mind and my soul reflect the infinite beauty of God's universe.*
>
> *I am stirred to creative action to utilize my gifts and talents to create something beautiful and enduring for all humanity. I am a channel for the expression of beauty. My personality now becomes magnetized with this image of beauty. My voice, my words, my facial expressions now echo this imprint of soul beauty that I wish to transmit to others. I become transfigured and I am attuned to the cosmic mind which now gives me flashes of inspiration and genius. I am now a true reflector of cosmic consciousness and all beauty, all good, all truth, all love and all peace are now transmitted to my higher creative brain centers for good.*

**How a Young Lady Became a Great Singer
through Meditation**

A young lady of my acquaintance wanted to become a singer. She had a fine, natural voice, but everyone told her that there was tremendous competition in that field and to forget her ambitions.

She learned of these laws of meditation and that anything is possible if one really believes it is. She began to meditate on beauty, not only in her personality, but in her voice and in her higher mind centers. She opened her consciousness to the loveliest sounds she could listen to. She listened to bird song at sunset. She became aware of the cricket's call in the fields when she walked. She stood beside the ocean and listened to the roar of the waves, as they caressed the seashore, until she could hear a veritable symphony made up of the surf, the wind and the silvery moonlight that made a pageant of beauty upon the sea.

Then this young lady began to listen to the greatest of all classical singers on recordings. She studied the lives of great composers and opera stars, until she was so filled with the cosmic consciousness of beauty that it instilled in her own voice its subtle overtones and echoes of infinite beauty.

When she went for an audition with a leading television station, she won out over twenty-five competitors and sang on one of the best musical shows on the air for many months.

2. The golden key of love when elevated to its highest plateau of creative action

To use this golden key of meditation to achieve cosmic consciousness go into the Beta state of meditation, in which your brain waves vibrate to from fourteen to twenty-eight cycles per second. This accelerated rate will tend to open higher centers of consciousness and cause you to become highly inspired.

This golden key of Love has been used by more thousands of people to achieve great creative power than any other emotion.

The telephone was created because Alexander Graham Bell wanted to create an instrument that would help his deaf wife hear again.

A man discovered the method for building tires for new automobiles because his wife was in a wheel chair and he wanted to find a substance that would make it easier to soften the shocks of motion when she went about in the chair.

The man who invented the mercury switch which brought him millions, was inspired by a desire not to awaken his wife at night with the clicking of the light switch.

Florence Nightingale elevated the profession of nursing because she loved humanity and went out on the battlefields to minister to wounded soldiers.

Cecil Rhodes founded his Rhodes Scholarship when he was healed of tuberculosis in Africa and discovered a diamond field; love of humanity was his inspiration.

Salk, Fleming, Pasteur, Nobel, Edison, Burbank, Booker-T. Washington, — all these great men and thousands more, were motivated by the divine emotion of love for humanity, and this divine emotion helped open mystic doors to cosmic consciousness.

Say or think the following words when you go into the Beta meditation to elevate love to its highest plateau of creative action:

> *I now meditate on the divine emotion of love with its many facets of creative action.*
>
> *I wish to create a happy and prosperous life for my family and friends. I elevate love to its highest plateau of creative action and desire cosmic consciousness so I may create according to the divine pattern of good, peace, joy and beauty.*
>
> *I now channelize the inspiring forces of divine love in my mind, my heart and my soul. I ask for the inner illumination of cosmic consciousness so I may radiate love to everyone I meet in my personality, my words and my actions.*

A woman I know, who lost her husband in an accident, was grief-stricken and did not know what she should do the rest of her life, until she learned about this meditation to re-kindle the creative power of love. She said this meditation every day for two weeks, until she was inspired to go into community social work, to help those who were sick and poor. She found new joy in this charitable impulse and stopped grieving for her husband.

A successful meditation for salesmen

I have given this meditation to salesmen, and they have reported to me that when they approached their work with the inspiration of creative love, they sold more of their products and had greater success.

Each day, several times a day, attune your mind to this creative emotion through meditation. You can meditate anywhere, even with your eyes wide open. All you need do is still your mind and then repeat the above meditation or one similar to it until you absorb its creative power. For hours you will feel its release of life power and creative energy.

**A housewife never tires because of
this meditation**

A housewife who complained to me of her daily burdens, said she was constantly fatigued. She cooked and cleaned for her husband and three children and at the end of the day she collapsed in exhaustion, too tired to even look at television. Her husband was beginning to tire of her constant complaints and her irritability and seemed less interested in her emotionally because she was chronically tired and could not share in simple little pleasures with him.

She used this meditation to release cosmic energy in her brain and body and several times a day she would stop her work, sit still for five minutes and say, "I am a channel for cosmic energy to flow through. I am inspired by love to create health and happiness for my husband and children. I am now charged with dynamic cosmic power to fulfill my day's tasks joyously." She soon became a dynamo of action and delighted her husband and children with her flow of creative energy and loving service.

**3. A desire to share your good with others
through charitable impulses**

This meditation helps release the frozen assets of your higher creative mind centers.

We all have tremendous capacity to create something great, but the fire of inspiration is often lacking. This can be created by having a desire to share your good with others.

For this meditation go into the Alpha state and think or say the following words:

I am now a channel for creative good. I meditate on the cosmic cornucopia of the universe from which pours an endless and inexhaustible supply of treasures for my good and for the good of others.

I am a cosmic center for peace and harmony. I now release peaceful thoughts to everyone I meet. I am joyous and I release my happiness and share it with everyone I meet.

I now pour the balm of harmony and love on the troubled waters of discord, enmity and friction, dissolving them and creating cosmic concord and harmony.

I give smiles, kindness and consideration and I am blessed

*with friendship. I forgive others for their unkind acts and I am
rewarded with love. I give service and labor and I receive riches
and rewards of abundance.*

How daily irritations were overcome

A woman I once knew told me she was always being cheated by
people. Salesmen and waiters short-changed her. Butchers gave her
the toughest cuts of meat. The fruit market gave her the hardest
peaches, the sourest oranges, the mealiest apples. She said, "Is there
something wrong with me that everyone tries to cheat me out of what
is rightfully mine?"

In talking to this woman for half an hour I found she lived perpetually in the consciousness of loss, limitation, lack and larceny.
People only reflected back to her what was in her consciousness.

I gave her this meditation for sharing her good with others, and told
her to use parts of it every time she approached anyone from whom
she wanted a fair deal. She began to practice the outgoing qualities
of the meditation, as well as the images of the benefits she was to
receive, and soon she found that people began to treat her better than
before.

4. The master motive to create prosperity, happiness and peace for all humanity

Cosmic Consciousness can be yours when you have the correct
master motives back of your life. One of the greatest of all master
motives is to create prosperity, happiness and peace for all humanity.

Most people live petty, selfish and mean little lives, in which they
are only concerned with self and family. When we expand the horizons
of our consciousness to embrace the cosmos and know we are all united
in bonds of spiritual brotherhood we become motivated by a different
emotion than selfishness — altruism, the desire to create prosperity,
health, happiness and peace for all humanity.

As you express a desire to create prosperity, happiness and peace,
you will open centers of consciousness that will bring you into align-
ment with the forces that make it possible for you to achieve these
conditions in your own life. Just as a magnet attracts to itself that
which vibrates in harmony with it, so too there is cosmic attraction
between elements that are in harmony with each other.

How Bitter Business Competition Was Healed

A man I once knew had a competitor in business who opened a store just across the street from him. He hated this man with intensity for he knew that his sales and profits would begin to go down. He began doing everything possible to cut prices, to put up big signs in his windows to lure the customers, but still the erosion of his profits continued.

In desperation this man sought me out. He had been to some of my lectures in Los Angeles, and remembered I had once said there are no competitors to us in our business. He asked me how he should handle this terrific problem that threatened his financial security.

I told him that the other man had a right to his security and his peace of mind, even though it might have seemed unfair to open a store in the same neighborhood. I then told him a meditation to use daily to help create an atmosphere of happiness and peace within himself:

> *There are no competitors in God's universe. My prosperity and good brings benefits to all people. I release my mind from concern over competition and create an atmosphere of peace, harmony and happiness in which I wish my competitor great success.*

I then told him to remove the big signs from his windows, to stop the price cutting, and bless the other man and his business every time he looked across the street.

He began to do this meditation, and very soon he noticed that customer's from the competitors shop, who had been attracted into the neighborhood looking for his products, began drifting across the street to his store. His attitude, now changed and outgoing, with thoughts of wanting to help others, impressed these new customers and they began buying more of his products than ever before!

Meditation to create prosperity, happiness and peace

I now open the centers of my consciousness to the influx of the spirit of co-operation and aid to others. I am now guided by the master motive to create prosperity, happiness and peace for others. I am in the consciousness of co-operation and my good will seek me out.

5. A desire to know God, to love him, and
bring His divine laws into expression

This last of our golden keys of meditation to open mystic doors to cosmic consciousness, is a very vital and important one. We are told, "For what shall it profit a man if he gain the whole world and lose his own soul?"

Cosmic Consciousness is achieved when we are able to align our own higher mind centers with the cosmic mind, which man calls God.

When this is achieved you will automatically have psychic unfoldment and cosmic perception, in which you will be guided unerringly to your true destiny.

In meditation for achieving this state of consciousness, sit quietly and let your mind be aware of the power of God in His universe. Meditate on the mystery back of life. See your soul as the chalice of the creative spirit, which is God.

Then, when you have achieved absolute stillness within and without, meditate as follows:

> *I now meditate on the reality of spirit and the unreality of matter. I know that I am a spiritual image of creative Father, consisting of mind, body and soul. I now claim my divine heritage and affirm my oneness with the infinite intelligence which is God. I now align my mind, body and soul with the infinite love, which God expresses. I now accept the mantle of infinite Good, which God releases. I now reflect His infinite peace and my life is peaceful and serene. I reflect His infinite beauty and my life becomes beautiful.*

When you have achieved oneness with the light, you will feel a sense of inner illumination. You will live under the spiritual laws to be found in the Ten Commandments, knowing that these are cosmic laws which help elevate man above the level of the jungle, into the spiritual stratosphere of love, forgiveness and charity.

You will live under the Golden Rule principle, knowing that what harms one will deprive others of security and happiness and that what blesses your life will in turn bless all humanity. You will apply the principles of the Sermon on the Mount, not because they are in some of the world's revealed religions, but because they are basic cosmic and universal laws which should be obeyed if we are to claim the sacred privileges that derive from spiritual knowledge and application

Review of Chapter Sixteen

1. How the great geniuses of history have used the mystic power of meditation to achieve cosmic consciousness and tap a strata of mental and spiritual power which was inspiring and illuminating.

2. How mystic meditation opened the doors of consciousness for great men like Newton and Beethoven, producing works of genius which have thrilled the world.

3. The five golden keys to mystic meditation that open doors to cosmic consciousness.

4. A desire to create something beautiful and enduring helps achieve cosmic consciousness.

5. A young lady became a great classical singer by using the meditation for achieving greatness and went on to win out over her competitors in a television program.

6. How to elevate the golden key of love to its highest plateau of creative action, and the meditation that helps you win this outstanding reward.

7. How eleven of the world's great geniuses used this meditation to achieve outstanding success, fame and fortune.

8. How a woman discovered new dimensions of life and became successful and happy as a social worker, when she used this meditation.

9. A housewife has learned to tap great cosmic energy and power, and never tires now in doing her work and serving her family.

10. How to achieve cosmic consciousness through a desire to share your good with others through charitable impulses.

11. How you may create prosperity, attain happiness and achieve peace of mind for yourself and others, by using this meditation for attaining cosmic consciousness.

12. A man used this meditation to promote better business relations and overcome his fear of a competitor.

13. How to use this meditation and attain cosmic consciousness, through a desire to know God, to love Him and to bring His divine laws into fullest expression.

HOW TO ACHIEVE
SPIRITUAL STRENGTH
AND COSMIC POWER
THROUGH MEDITATION

17

Your soul is on a mystical journey through time and space in a search for the magnificent life.

In its brief adventure on this earth, in the physical body, the soul knows suffering and pain, ecstasy and love. The entire purpose for living is not just to meet life's challenges and overcome them so we may know happiness, but it is so that the soul may achieve the spiritual grandeur and absolute cosmic power to rise triumphantly above life's challenges.

In this chapter we shall learn how this can be achieved through the power of transcendental meditation.

On this mystical quest through time and space, the soul is guided by a divine ray of light, which issues from the cosmic mind of God. This higher intelligence focuses in man's consciousness, when he attunes himself to the spiritual forces of life. He is then intuitively guided to the finding of his higher self, and the thrilling spiritual experience which gives him dynamic purposefulness and cosmic awareness of his true magnificent destiny.

When your soul obeys these higher promptings of the cosmic intelligence, it invariably seeks out the right life experiences that it needs to fulfill its destiny perfectly.

THE BELIEF IN REINCARNATION

Two-thirds of the people on earth believe that the soul has lived before and will live again, in a continuous life experience that spans many lifetimes. There are many astounding proofs which seem to signify that this is true.

The Christian dispensation believed in reincarnation for many years. This belief was eliminated from the Christian faith when Emperor Constantine announced he would accept Christianity if all references to reincarnation were deleted. Soul-survival and return were taught by Christ and these teachings have spread throughout the world, giving the weight of evidence to this ancient belief of reincarnation.

To better understand reincarnation, it is necessary to know that it is tied in with the law of Karma. In each lifetime the soul builds merits or demerits, according to an individual's actions. The more merits one builds the less Karmic debt a person accumulates, and the less often he returns to this physical plane of suffering, sickness, pain and death. When the soul has built sufficient merits it can wipe out the Karmic debts that have been accumulated over the centuries, and then the soul may continue to other planes of consciousness and receive its spiritual rewards.

This idea of punishments or rewards is similar to the present Christian belief in heaven and hell. One is punished for evil Karma and rewarded for good Karma. The theory of reincarnation teaches that man creates his own heaven or hell, and he is rewarded or punished by his own deeds in successive lifetimes.

WHERE DOES THE SOUL GO AFTER DEATH?

There are many theories about where the soul goes after death. In our solar system and in the galaxies beyond, science now knows there are billions and even trillions of planets where existence is continued indefinitely in many forms that are totally different from that on earth. Science estimates that of these billions of planets at least one hundred million of them are capable of sustaining life. The soul's existence is possible in another dimension of time and space, in what reincarnationists call Nirvana, where the soul dwells in eternal splendor in the presence of the God-head from which it issued.

In this cosmic or divine romance that the soul enters it discovers the eternal bliss that comes when the lover and beloved come into the state of perpetual ecstasy known as Nirvana.

When life's lessons have been learned, the soul need not return to a gross, physical body of flesh, subject to pain, sickness, age and death. The soul then ascends to its rightful domain of spiritual grandeur, having fulfilled its potentials of absolute peace, absolute love, absolute joy and absolute power.

METHOD FOR ACHIEVING THE SOUL'S SPIRITUAL STRENGTH

1. Each day enter into a state of deep meditation in which you carefully examine all the facets of soul experiences you have in life. See life as a spiritual experience, not physical. Meditate on the reality of God, the soul, the mystery back of life. Say the following words in this deep spiritual meditation:

> *I now meditate on the meaning and mystery of life. I recognize the source of my origin as being spiritual not physical and material. I now contemplate the mystery of my physical body. Born in the bonds of spiritual love, I have embarked upon a mystical journey through time and space. My soul inhabits a body that is physical and subject to the laws of erosion. I now contemplate the mystery of my soul. I am aware of God and His infinite Presence within me. I am aware of the true spiritual purpose of my existence. I was created to evolve my consciousness and to release the hidden splendor of my soul. I now meditate on the Karmic pattern of events that I shall institute to lead me to a finding of the grandeur of the true cosmic and spiritual experiences of life. I am attuned to love and my soul is elevated to the noblest expression of this divine emotion. I am attuned to Joy, and my soul is bathed in vibrations of intense happiness. I am in tune with Good and my soul strives to be aware of all that is good and Godly. I am in an atmosphere of peace and my soul is at peace with the world. I attune myself to the higher octaves of infinite beauty and my soul registers all sights and sounds and experiences that attest to the cosmic splendour of the God-power which created me in beauty.*

How a Troubled Soul Changed Her Destiny with this Meditation

A woman came to me for counselling once who was troubled by a series of catastrophes and soul-shattering events that left her bewildered and broken in spirit. She wailed, "Why is God punishing me? What have I done that I should be made to suffer so miserably?"

After listening to her tragic story I knew what soul Karma she had built and that in this lifetime her Karma had caught up with her and she was punishing herself.

She had been married three times, and each time, for various reasons she had been divorced. Her three children had been lost to her through her neglect and drinking. She had sunk so low that no man would marry her and give her security. On top of this she had taken to various forms of dope addiction and her mind and body were tormented repeatedly when she was put into institutions to overcome this habit.

I gave this woman spiritual therapy, in which she was put on a daily regimen of many different forms of positive action. But the main thing, after I had her confidence, I put her on the above spiritual meditation, to show her the purpose and value of life and that there was hope for her spiritually if she believed in the power of God and let it redeem her life.

She had once been religious and she now returned to her own church. She began to use the transcendental meditations every day, and whenever she felt the need of dope or drink, she went into deep meditation until the desire passed. Soon she was able to go for days without stimulants and then her troubled soul was healed and she began to come out of her deep despondency and bewilderment. Within two months time this woman was on a different soul-path from formerly and I see her from time to time and encourage her to continue her spiritual progress towards enlightenment.

The necessity of Keeping in Tune

2. Daily attune your soul to the divine attributes which bring spiritual grandeur and nobility to the life experience.

A violin, when out of tune, can make hideous sounds. When it is perfectly tuned it makes sweet music. I once visited one of the world's greatest violinists backstage, when I was lecturing in Carnegie Hall. This great violinist owned a Stradivarius worth over a million dollars. He was walking back and forth in his dressing room playing scales on it, when suddenly the violin made the most discordant sounds I had ever heard! I exclaimed in astonishment, thinking something had happened to his precious violin. He turned to me with a laugh and showed me that he had loosened the pegs of the violin, making it deliberately go out of tune. "Even a million dollar violin cannot make beautiful music when it is out of tune." He told me. Then he once again tuned it correctly and beautiful sounds poured forth from the seasoned, old instrument. He went out onto the stage and thrilled three thousand people with his heavenly music!

The instrument of your mind and soul can only make sweet music when you attune yourself to great and noble thoughts and ideas.

Each day of your life, when you begin your day, go into this cosmic meditation to attune your mind and soul to the music of the spheres:

> *I now meditate on the highest and noblest concepts that my mind can conceive. I know that I am created in the image and likeness of God and that my soul partakes of His beauty and perfection. I now elevate my consciousness to lofty and inspiring planes of action. I idealize my thoughts and actions, striving to achieve idealism in all my relations with others. I practice honesty and truth in my daily life. I forgive others for what they have done to me and I ask forgiveness for my moral infractions of spiritual and cosmic laws. I show mercy and compassion to others and refuse to cast the first stone. I strive to be charitable and kind, sharing my good with others. I am now in holy communion with the cosmic spirit that animates the universe and I am blessed by all the forces of good in my daily life experience.*"

3. Accept life's challenges as part of the soul discipline needed to strengthen you for greater glory. To give you this soul strength to meet life's various problems use this daily meditation:

> *I recognize the need of problems and struggles to give me soul growth and spiritual evolvement. I meet these challenges with courage, faith and hope. I know that I am spiritually strengthened when I face and overcome life's problems. My soul is now charged with dynamic spiritual power which brings me peace of mind and peace of soul.*

4. To grow spiritually and evolve the soul to heights of grandeur and nobility, each day dedicate your life to God and doing good. Go into meditation for five minutes after you awaken and think or say the following:

> *Today I dedicate my thoughts and deeds to God. I dedicate my breath and my words to His greater glory. I speak words of beauty and joy, communicating an atmosphere of harmony and wonder to every one I meet. I thank God for the gift of life and the opportunity of serving Him.*

5. Each day search out soul experiences in your life that will add to spiritual grandeur. Sift out of each day's varied activities those experiences that elevate and inspire your mind and soul. Refuse to see the shabby, tawdry, ugly and disturbing things that are all around you and focus your higher mind on only those soul experiences that add to your elevation of consciousness over the earthbound forces of life. Use this meditation for that purpose:

> *I see all beauty as a reflection of God's infinite presence in His creation. I am attuned to the beauty of nature, the mountains and oceans, the trees and flowers, the silvery moon and golden sun, the myriad stars that bedeck the purple veil of nigh . I enthrone this grandeur in my mind and soul and I am elevated to lofty planes of consciousness.*
>
> *I hear all truth, and know that it is a cosmic reflection of the voice of God, speaking eloquently in the whispering wind through the treetops; the carolling of birds in their nests; the cascading of waterfalls as they flow to the cosmic seas; the happy laughter of little children, attesting to purity, innocence and Godliness. I am in tune with the joy and wonder of the cosmos and my soul is elevated to supernal heights of revelation and wisdom.*

How Frustration of a 60-Year Old Man Was Healed

A man had become so caught up in the humdrum things of life that he was bitter and disillusioned. He told me he had no purpose in living. "I am sixty years old, my wife is dead, my children are grown up and don't need me. I sometimes think it would be better to be dead," he lamented. This man had put into the cosmic memory bank of his consciousness only thoughts of misery, discontent and tragedy. He had lost his inspiration for living.

I put him back on the spiritual track of life by giving him a regimen which included the following: Each day meditate on the true meaning of your life. See the glories of the world, not the failures. Realize you have lived a full life of beauty and have achieved love-fulfillment, the rearing of a wonderful family. Now spend the rest of your life giving God thanks for the miracles you have enjoyed for sixty years Stop seeing the minus signs of life and see all the plusses that you have. I gave him this meditation to use, and this man became remark- ably tranquil and changed. He even improved in health, for as hioutlook changed from negative to positive, his glands were given an impetus to life, not death, and he prospered and later became interested in a widow that he now plans to marry!

6. Each day of your life reflect divine harmony, order and balance. The mind and spirit of man cannot evolve in an atmosphere of discord and friction. Your soul thrives on peace and serenity. Each day when you are faced with turbulence in your own home or business environment, stop for a moment and say or think the following meditation for soul harmony:

> *I was created in bonds of peace and concord. I now go back into the peaceful womb of time and am reborn in spirit. I am immune to life's discords and am surrounded by the magic circle of God's protective love. I am one with cosmic order and harmony and I attract into my orbit of experience only serenity, joy and peace.*

7. Have as your life goal, not just making money and having material success and riches and abundance, but a higher motivation back of your life. Release the creative spirit of inspiration and ultimate betterment for all mankind. Set a goal of universal brotherhood, overcoming of war and establishing of peace, educational standards that are lofty and universal. Meditate each day on the highest ideals you can imagine, and see cosmic unity between all God's creatures. Express divine love to everyone you meet and your soul will be given a new impetus towards Godliness.

8. Remove the Karmic debts that you may have accumulated in past lives through a strict adherence to spiritual laws that have been enunciated by all the great Mystics, Seers, Teachers and Prophets and which are revealed in all the world's nine religions. These spiritual laws are given in the Ten Commandments, in the Golden Rule, and the Sermon On The Mount.

9. Each day, as the ultimate form of meditation, be in prayerful communication with the Cosmic Spirit which manifests in all creation. When you awaken in the morning, let a prayer be on your lips; a prayer of gratitude for another day of life, and the opportunity to serve God and humanity.

Review of Points in Chapter Seventeen

The soul searches for ultimate fulfillment in this mystical

journey through time and space and must find the divine ray of light for ultimate spiritual completion.

2. The belief in reincarnation and how it shows the soul pattern through successive lifetimes.

3. Man's soul searches for Nirvana, in which it finds the eternal divine romance and the soul merges with the Divine Source of its origin.

4. Meditation to establish the soul's contact with the source of its power and to reveal the mystery in which it is caught up.

5. How a woman changed her destiny from one of tragedy and bewilderment to peace of mind and peace of soul through using a deep spiritual meditation daily.

6. How you can discover the spiritual grandeur and nobility of life by attuning your mind and soul to great and noble thoughts and ideas.

7. The challenges of life are sent to you for soul discipline and to strengthen you for future glory. How you can use meditation to achieve absolute spiritual power.

8. The daily experiences of life should add to the spiritual grandeur of your soul. This is achieved through meditation on the beauty, truth, good and love that surround you in life.

9. How a sixty-year old man overcame bitterness and disillusionment through a meditation that gave him a new purpose in living.

10. Your life can reflect divine harmony, order and balance each day. These are the cosmic forces by which the soul finds unison with the positive elements of life.

11. How to remove the karmic debts accumulated over many lifetimes and achieve soul growth through the spiritual laws to be found in all great religions.

74 75 10 9 8 7 6 5 4 3 2 1